MEN OF AFRICAN DESCENT OVERCOMING SOCIAL EXCLUSION

Black Men's Forum 1998 National Conference Report

Edited by Carl Hylton

LEEDS METROPOLITAN UNIVERSITY

BMF

Black Men's Forum 1998 National Conference Report

MEN OF AFRICAN DESCENT OVERCOMING SOCIAL EXCLUSION

Edited by Carl Hylton

First published in 1999 by Gbakhanda Publishing,
Leeds Metropolitan University and the Black Men's Forum

ISBN 1 874555 01 X

Cover picture: Paul Auber, 1995 (Musa Suma and Leslie Bernard)
Design by Delroy Goodison and Carl Hylton

For further copies of this report, please send a cheque for £5 (plus £1 p&p) made payable to Black Men's Forum, to:
Black Men's Forum, Chapeltown Enterprise Centre, 231 Chapeltown Road, Leeds, LS7 3DX. Telephone: 0113 262 6333

Black Men's Forum 1998 conference speakers, organisers and delegates.
Pictures by St. Clair Brown and Luke Daniels.

Top centre: Robert Pitt (right).
Top right: Patrice Naiambana.
Middle right: St. Clair Brown (left), Carl Hylton, Trevor Gordon,
                      Molefi Kete Asante and Claude Hendrickson.

Contents

1

Tribute to Musa Suma

In memory of brother Musa Suma who died on 29 January 1999

Musa was born in Samu in Guinea, West Africa in 1939.

In his late teens, after a French-Arabic education and an apprenticeship with Ballets Africans, he moved to neighbouring Sierra Leone where he worked as a lorry driver until his drumming and painting was recognised and led to a job as a drummer with the Sierra Leone National Dance Troupe.

Musa toured extensively in Africa with the Troupe, also visiting countries in Asia and Europe.

A lifelong friend of the internationally acclaimed West African dramatists Yulisa Amadu Maddy, Musa played a pivotal role in the musical productions of Maddy's Gbakanda African Tiata Company, a role which brought him to Leeds, with the company in 1986.

Soon after a successful one-year residency with Gbakanda in Leeds, Musa developed kidney failure and started dialysis three times a week at Leeds Infirmary. With a young family to support and unable to return to Sierra Leone, Musa took up English Literacy classes and began to develop his career as a artist, enjoying exhibitions and sales in Birmingham, Liverpool, Doncaster, Leeds.

As a pioneering drummer and musician Musa worked in schools and colleges, and led workshops all over Britain. A widely respected and popular Master Drummer, Musa performed and tutored at several annual festivals, including Leeds Rhythms of the City, the Bristol based British Drumming Convention, Drum Call and the Glastonbury Festival.

Musa is survived by Megan, and children Kadiatu, Sheriff, Mabinty and Esta (Auber, 1999, 6).

A MAN OF DIGNITY, INTEGRITY AND PURPOSE

Acknowledgements

The work of emotional and economic community regeneration takes many forms, one aspect being this conference report. To arrive at this stage involves the commitment and collaboration of many people inside and outside the community of people of African descent. The most important of these people are the speakers and delegates who attended the Black Men's Forum's national conference on 31 October 1998. I also wish to highlight the conference planning group, caterers, Maureen Wilkes and her team, crèche workers, Tessa Frances and Alene Paul, and Angela and Patrica Benjamine who organised the conference registration at the West Yorkshire Playhouse. Special thanks to Ken Brown for allowing us to display a selection of his treasured paintings, stall holders, Tony Crawford from Black Community Aids Team based in Leeds, and Al Barnett from Berry Edwards Books based in Manchester.

The conference report was improved by contributions and comments from Eli Anderson, Molefi Kete Asante, Paul Auber, St. Clair Brown, Andy Forbes, Urban Muhammad, Patrice Naiambana, Paul Obinna, Omari, Lakhbir Virk, Calvin Wilkes, Nigel Williams, Trevor Gordon, Claude Hendrickson and Nat Lindo.

Counsellor Norman Hutchingson, Yasmin Hussein (Leeds Central Equal Opportunity Department), Mohsin Zulfiqar (Equality Language and Learning Agency) and Lakhbir Virk (Centre for Race, Culture and Education, Leeds Metropolitan University), were quick to grasp the important significance of the conference event, and helped to provide moral and financial support to enable this important report to be published.

Black Men's Forum conference planning group

Conference planning group

Paul Auber	Community Development Consultant
Cleveland Bertram	Chel, Resourcing the Community
St. Clair Brown	Chapeltown Community Centre
Clinton Cameron	Chapeltown and Harehills Enterprise Limited (Chel) Community Trust
Stephen Derek	Phoenix Dance Company
Topher Campbell	West Yorkshire Playhouse
Claude Hendrickson	Chapeltown 10-2 Club and Chel
Ali Hussein	Hall Place Studies, Leeds Metropolitan University
Carl Hylton	Research Consultant
Edric James	Mary Seacole Halfway House
Robert Pitt	Press Officer
Calvin Wilkes	Chapeltown Enterprise Centre
Vince Wilkinson	Open University (Yorkshire Region)
Jerome Williams	Technical Advisor

Conference sponsors

Centre for Ethnicity and Racism Studies, University of Leeds
Chapeltown and Harehills Enterprise Limited (Chel) Community Trust
Commission for Racial Equality
Joseph Rowntree Charitable Trust
Leeds Joint Planning Support Unit – Community Chest
Leeds Metropolitan University
Manningham Housing Association
Multicultural Education Consultancy Advisory Services (MECAS)
Open University (Yorkshire Region)
Sadehlok Housing Association
The Voice
United Caribbean Association
Unity Housing Association
West Yorkshire Playhouse

The conference was video taped by Ali Hussein and Derek Evelyn, audio tape recorded by Ansel Broderick, and transcribed by Beverley Freeman

Introduction and summary

Background

The past five years have seen the growth of local community discussions involving men of African descent in many UK cities and towns. The emergence of these Black Male Forums and other projects that target males of African descent, are progressive group actions to encourage men to use their own efforts to pull themselves up beside women of African descent. Men require grassroots action because of their economic, social and political exclusion from many areas of mainstream UK society. In comparison, women of African descent are sure and assertive, involved in local community groups, further education and professional occupations (Hylton, 1999, 55-72).

In this quiet inner city revolution, men in Bradford, Birmingham, Leeds, London, Manchester, Nottingham, Oxford and Sheffield, have set up projects that target males of African descent. The Leeds Black Men's Forum is a key organisation in this changing environment. On Saturday 31 October 1998 they organised a conference at the West Yorkshire Playhouse which brought together one hundred representatives of men's groups from across the UK. This is a report of that event entitled, *Men Of African Descent Overcoming Social Exclusion,* with discussion led by eminent Africancentric academic and activist Dr. Molefi Kete Asante, who is Professor at Temple University, USA, and London based educationalist, Trevor Gordon. Key areas of national concern are issues about education, training, employment, and the spiritual well-being of themselves, family and community. Assisted by music and cultural performances from African Master Drummer Musa Suma and Royal Shakespeare Company actor Patrice Naiambana, conference delegates resolved to maintain contacts, continue to share information and work on further practical initiatives.

The 1998 national conference built on a previous event in 1997, *Black Men in Britain: Marching into the Millennium* (Hylton [ed.], 1997a). Men were inspired by the Million Man March that took place in Washington DC in October 1995. They are also aware that boys of African descent are five times more likely to be excluded from school than other children - that males of African descent are disproportionly involved in mental health services - and more than half of men of African descent under twenty-five years old are unemployed.

Male actions such as the Leeds Black Men's Forum is in the tradition of direct action and self-help initiatives that have been the hallmark of African-Caribbean community activities. In the coming years there is no doubt that these grassroots projects will grow into powerful forces for change. Men of African descent are determined to build positive environments where they and their families and community can thrive.

Leeds Black Men's Forum aims

- To raise awareness of the challenges faced by individual men of African descent.
- To research, analyse and discuss methods of creating strong individuals, families and communities.
- To challenge the negative and disabling stereotypes ascribed to men of African descent.
- To make links and network with other forums of men of African descent, and forums of other ethnic groups consisting of males and females, for the purpose of disseminating information.
- To help create and establish forums for men of African descent where there are none, or when requested to do so.·
- To raise the awareness of individuals, and voluntary and statutory organisations that can support the above goals (Black Men's Forum, 1998).

Conference programme
Our history and strength as men of African descent
- African drumming - Musa Suma
- Welcome address by chair Claude Hendrickson
- Dr. Molefi Kete Asante
- Questions and discussion
- Trevor Gordon
- Questions and discussion

LUNCH

Where are we now - Black men's forum organisations
- Marimba playing - Musa Suma
- Dramatic performance - Patrice Naiambana
- Local male forum representatives
- Questions and open discussion

The future
- Open discussion - the way forward
- Summary and close

The layout of this report closely follows the conference programme. Prior to the start of the discussion there was an African drumming 'wake up call' from Master African Drummer, Musa Suma, followed by one minute's silence to commemorate the death of brother Steven Lawrence.

Leeds based Musa Suma who died three months after the conference, was a gifted musician and visual artist widely respected throughout West Africa and the UK.

The event was introduced and chaired by a renown Black Men's Forum and Leeds activist, Claude 'Hopper' Hendrickson. He is perhaps best known as the co-ordinator of Frontline Self-Build Housing Association, which was the first Black self-build housing co-operative in the North of England. He is now involved in the Leeds based, YES-Cyber Project, a one-stop-shop, providing an information technology, education, housing and employment surgery with internet access, for young people in Chapeltown and Harehills.

The first conference session, *Our history and strength as men of African descent*, introduced key speakers, Dr. Molefi Kete Asante and Trevor Gordon.

8

Molefi Kete Asante is Professor of African American Studies at Temple University, Philadelphia, USA. He is an internationally renown Africancentric academic and community activist with forty-two books and more than two hundred scholarly articles to his credit. Creator of the first doctoral program in African American Studies, he has lectured throughout the world on issues of African culture, philosophy and the structure of knowledge in the western world.

Molefi, a gifted speaker, concentrated on expressing the fundamental basis of the Afrocentric philosophy he has done so much to influence. He addressed issues such as parenting and the creation of initiation ceremonies as means of knowing and giving due praise and respect to African ancestors. He also provided examples of appropriate cultural curricula for people of African descent (especially boys), and went on to argue for the creation of independent cultural institutions of people of African descent, as a method to instil cultural esteem.

Trevor Gordon is head of Community Development at Lambeth College in London. He is a Freelance Education Consultant with particular expertise concerning issues of social exclusion, equality of opportunity and strategies for inclusion. He is also a passionate school exclusion appeal advocate, and his research works and practice have led to the publication of several education articles.

Trevor Gordon seized the opportunity to deliver a thoughtful presentation, which main focus dealt with the obstacles to overcome before effective African male organisations can be built and sustained. The key issues he outlined were: men's lack of self-awareness, the need to reject focusing on class, caste or shade, brotherly support rather than envy and 'bad mouthing', respect for women, and the making of 'serious' family commitments to children and partners.

After lunch the second conference session, *Where are we now - Black men's forum organisation,* began with scintillating Marimba playing from Musa Suma. This was followed by a sketch dialogue by performing artist Patrice Naiambana using the characterisation of a fictional African leader, General Alfred Providence Mukata, exiled in the UK after a coup. With a skilful blend of wit and humour in-tune with the experiences of his audience, he explored the difficulties of creating and sustaining African self-government within a climate of western hypocrisy and cultural, financial and political influences. The implications for independent cultural survival for diasporian Africans were also investigated.

Patrice Naiambana is a performing artist, writer, producer and musician. One of his most recent television appearances was the lead role in the Channel 4 sitcom, *In Exile*. He is now working at the Royal Shakespeare Company. Patrice is the founder of Tribal Soul, which uses community theatre as an educational tool. He was also the key instigator of the People's Arts Council (PAC), an arts collective based in Chapeltown, Leeds.

Following these important arts based cultural events were representatives of various male organisations who shared their group experiences. Chris Thomas and Nigel Guy from the Nubian Men's Group based in Bradford, informed conference delegates about their mis-treatment by the police at the Steven Lawrence Enquiry, and the group's commitment to overcome the difficulties between African men of different generations. Nat Lindo from Huddersfield's A. F. R. I. C. A. Project gave an overview of his work to 'try to raise the [school] achievement level of Black African-Caribbean young people'. Godfrey Muhammad represented the Nation of Islam Northern Regional Study Guide Group based in Huddersfield. He indicated the urgent need to get in touch with our African self to create our own reality rather than building a reality created by others. Similar to other speakers he was unconcerned about being socially excluded from a UK society that is deceitful, immoral and unjust. Eli Anderson and Nigel Williams from London's Waltham Forest Youth Service, gave an overview about the difficulties of developing a conference for young men of African descent. The work around the event is designed as a foundation to increase their life-skills. Andy Forbes and Paul Obinna from the Manchester based Iroko Group gave powerful presentations concerning the need to start the individual and group building process from within. They emphasised a 'grounding' and reconnection with African spiritual female and male traditions and power. Rupert Beverley from Indaba, based in Huddersfield, was also concerned with the self-healing aspects of group discussions. The final presentation in this conference session was made by St. Clair Brown on behalf of the Black Men's Forum and the conference organising group based in Leeds. He talked about the changing environment and possibilities

10

for progressive change for men of African descent, and indicated the need to keep women of African descent informed of ongoing action plans. Following on closely from these presentations, the final session, *The future,* was a free-flowing discussion involving all conference delegates.

Main outcomes

The main outcomes of the conference was a sharing of knowledge and feeling of solidarity, with renewed emphasis to continue with practical schemes for change. Delegates failed to plan a collective effort for change although they were clear about the concerns that required attention. These were as follows: acquiring self-knowledge, regaining cultural esteem, emphasis on self-sufficiency, development of a changed relationship with women, children and other members of their African family, acknowledgement and support of other people of African descent, creation of independent cultural institutions, use of collective energies rather than individual activity, creation of initiation ceremonies and honouring ancestors, rejection of class and caste, and finally, the importance of education.

Our history and strength as men of African descent

Drumming by African Master Drummer - **Musa Suma**

Conference chair	**Claude Hendrickson**	Leeds

Hello, good morning - that was Musa Suma giving you the Wake Up Call. My name is Claude Hendrickson. I'm a member of the Black's Men's Forum, and obviously I'm here to welcome you. The second item on today's agenda will be a minute's silence ... in remembrance of Stephen Lawrence.

We're here today, number one, to celebrate a year since the last conference, which we also had here. We're also here to share knowledge with other groups, ... to go on to be the foundation for ... [a] national organisation ... [or] forum which can meet on a regular basis.

[Let me say] a little bit more about the Black Men's Forum. The Forum is made up of local Black men in Chapeltown ... who got together obviously because of the negative views about Black males. ... [We wanted to focus on] Black male achievements, where we wanted to be and where we wanted to go, and to look into where we may be beyond the millennium. Last year's conference was kind of successful - this book [Black Men in Britain: Marching into the Millennium, (Hylton (ed.), 1997a)] came out of this conference, and is available outside for anybody to purchase - so if you haven't got your own copy make sure you get one before you leave.

We have two very prestigious, important speakers [here today, one] from the US, [and] one from here in London. [They are] going to give you a good spiel - remembering that the speakers are here not to lead us anywhere but to encourage us on the road that we are about to travel. The first up is from the United States, Dr. Molefi Kete Asante. There's so many things [to say] about him - he's written forty-two books, he works with schools and colleges, he's on the radio, and he takes young Black American kids to Egypt every year. ... He flew into the country a couple of days ago. He's here to share his knowledge with all of you, and to answer questions - so I'd like to introduce straight away, up front - Dr. Molefi Asante.

An orientation to a manhood discussion

I come in peace! Habari gana? What's the news? Hotep! Peace! The first greeting is a Swahili greeting, the second is an ancient Kemetic greeting. Whenever a speaker stands before an audience of brothers he should be in peace, otherwise he appears as an enemy to himself. So I say again, I come in peace!

When we come together like this we should remember our ancestors because very early in our own history as people we honoured the ancestors. This was tradition. It was the practice of the Nile Valley philosophers, and it has been carried on as a tradition throughout Africa from that ancient time.

So African men gathered here in Leeds represent a continuation of the ancestors. We are not covering only new material - we are on old grounds and have to appreciate the foundation that has been laid for us. All praise is due to the great god Ra, the supreme creator. To Ptah, Ogun, Chukwu, Yemanja, Ausar, Auset, Heru, and all the names of our spirituality, the neters nefer, the beautiful gods - I always give thanks. Let's get right to it - all spirituality is about centring, and it is very basic to the concept and the idea of African manhood. I have been given thirty minutes to hold a conversation with you. I'll talk real fast and hope that you get the gist of what it is that I have to say.

Afrocentricity and Africanity

First of all as you know you probably heard my philosophical orientation is as an Afrocentrist. What that means essentially ... [is] that African people should act in our own interest - that we should not only act in our own interest, we should also view reality from the standpoint of our own centredness rather than as victims, or as objects in the European world view. ... Essentially we act out of our own interest ... as self-determining humans. There is no one in the world who is better able to operate or to act for African people or for African men than Africans themselves.

14

The Afrocentrist believes ... fundamentally in the subject place of African men, not that we are somehow imitation whites - and there are a lot of whites who would like to believe that, or like to think that. But in African thought we are ourselves, our own best examples. ... This is not the same as Africanity. Some people say: 'you know the Afrocentrist means that you have to change your name to an African name, wear African clothes and go to Africa'. No, that's Africanity, that's different. Afrocentricity is a self-conscious act. It is highest level of action that an African can have because it means in whatever capacity you are in, every situation at all times as an African man, you act in the best interest of African people. ... [This is] the fundamental theme that I have in terms of institution building, in terms of ... our relationships to African women, in terms of how we respond to our children. The whole fundamental basis is African acting in the interest of African people.

Cultural curricula
... I come with greetings but I come to tell you that the story in the US is about like the story here. We have a population of African-Americans in the US, which is about 13% of the population of the country. ... About 6% of the population ... [are] African males, but 40% of all prisoners in the US are African males - and we have two million African males who cannot vote in the elections because of criminal records. So the criminalisation of the African male in the US begins very early - in fact it begins in school. It begins when the child is nine or ten years old. ... A recent study [found] that in school districts where you have a majority of African children in the classroom and a majority of white teachers, you have a higher rate of school students getting into difficulty than in the school districts where you have a higher percentage of Black children, but you have a higher percentage of Black teachers. Which means therefore that somehow there is a problem between white teachers and Black children, particularly Black males at nine or ten years of age. We are now trying to redress that problem and to redress the problem of the curriculum itself, because we think that Black men are very early chosen by the school system in a way that puts them on a track to prison.

First thing they say is that Black children are too active, Black male children are too physical. What do you mean too physical? It means that other children are just not physical. Why do you say our children are too physical, what do you mean by that - explain it? ... So what we've had to do is devise curricula that would take advantage of the cultural style of Black children - so if they are too physical, then instead of having just your regular Eurocentric singing group, then have a drama ensemble. Let the young brothers play drums, you can do that in a classroom - there's nothing wrong with that. You got to sing in groups why don't you have them in drumming groups if you have other activities for other children. If ... [some groups are] playing chess, well then let these [Black] children play some kind of activity, if you are talking about energy. So part of what we've had to do is to look at the styles of African children, particularly African male children, because the first thing that they do is simply say that: 'this child does not fit this situation'. Well we say: 'these teachers don't fit these children'.

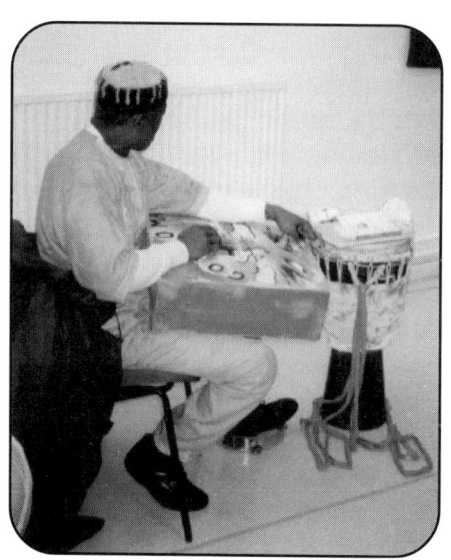

Musa Suma

Picture by St. Clair Brown

16

Chosen people

Look, we are chosen people, you know that - that's why you're here - you chose [to be here]. What does it mean to be a chosen person? It means you are self-choosing - that's all it means. If you're not self-choosing you ain't chosen. The only chosen people in the world are self-choosing people. If you do not choose to save your own children - if you do not say: 'we choose ourselves' - then you will never be chosen. The only way that Black men, African men, can be chosen is for us to continue that process. Let me give you in the time that I have, several points that I think may be useful here in the UK as you begin this process of continuing the maintenance of the ... psychological, the cultural, the spiritual [and] economic health of Black men. First of all I think that you are now in a position ... to create more of your own institutions. ... There shouldn't be any reason why white people believe that they have to come to every meeting you have. ... If you have a meeting, they gotta come, they got to be there. There shouldn't be any reason for that - you don't have to go to all their meetings - but you have to have your own institutions to do that. If you don't have your own institutions you can never control that situation, you can't even talk to each other in a family way. ... Other people who are not part of the family come in and hear what you're talking about, and go right out, and before you get into the process of trying to do something positive for your community, you are already undermined. You do not bring into any discussion about your family, other people - you can't do that. We learnt that a long time ago in the US, that's why the most positive thing that we have ... (I think, this is one of the things we bring) - is organisation. When we say African organisation, we mean African organisation.

... The first thing you got to build is institutions, even if they are small institutions, ... if there's [only] one room. ... If we need to have this conference in somebody's house, let's do that, because that's the only way you can be free, otherwise you have no freedom. See I'm talking from experience, I don't know the UK experience but I'm telling you what happened in the US.

17

That's fundamental - we built organisations - we built organisations a long time. A lot of the time we had to build because of segregation. ... You see the brother who played the beautiful drums - you know what white folks used to say when we played drums? They thought we were playing war music - we were - that's what it is - and they got scared of the drums and said: 'you can't play drums in here - you can play the piano, but you can't play drums'. You know what I'm saying because part of it is a cultural situation. When you start talking in-house about what you need to do in terms of institution building, you are talking about how you work towards the interest of self-determination. Within any western industrial society you gonna have racism and you gonna have white supremacy - that is a fundamental reality. So white people operate in their own best interest, and even when they operate with you they operate in their own best interests. This is why there are certain kinds of attitudes and ideas ... that you can't even discuss because they have this whole notion that you are simply imitating them. ... Well I'm not an imitator - I'm in great opposition to white supremacy. I am a living reality. It's my life mission to undermine it every opportunity I get, because it has undermined African people - undermined African sensibility, created havoc, racism, and destruction in the world.

Self-esteem or cultural esteem
This is not about self-pride - African people don't need any self-esteem building, ... we have the self-esteem we need - we've always had self-esteem. ... You ask any African person in this room - we like how we look - how we dance - how we play music. We like who we are - that's not a problem - what we don't like is, we don't like Africa. So it's not a problem with self-esteem, it's a problem with cultural esteem and the problem with not liking Africa. [This] is also the direct result of white supremacy, because people have told us negative things about Africa.

Hard work, struggle and generosity

I take the position that no one can out-work you - no one can out-achieve African people. This is why people work so hard to keep you down. That's why they won't give you jobs. They know that African people are very hard working. I say work hard, but fight if necessary.

The reason I say fight if necessary is because I don't take the position that African people should be pushovers to anybody. I'm not a pushover - I don't believe in being a pushover. If you don't impose your will on others, they will impose their will on you. It is a record of the world. You've got to teach your children to be strong. I teach my son strength is extremely important, but our ancestors also knew courtesy and generosity - these are our traits. I like the way the Mossi people do it in Burkina Faso. Every Friday the king has a ritual, and he comes out dressed in a red outfit, and then of course he goes back in, and he comes out, and he is dressed in a white outfit, and he says: 'if you're ready for war, we're ready for war, if you're ready for peace we're ready for peace'. That's the way African people have always been, but you can't allow people to impose on you all the time because ... [they] recognise that you will not fight back, and if you don't fight back then you will always be a loser. You can't do that - that's not in our history - that's not even in our tradition. ... Yet in society where you have white supremacy as the ideology of that society it becomes extremely difficult for African people to be themselves.

Another issue to remember is don't just work for money, work for the interest of the community. ... If you work for the interest of the community what you are doing then is building the community, you are creating an attitude, an atmosphere of success. If you work with the attitude that you are raising the spiritual level of the community, then your work takes on a greater capacity to bring good in a collective sense - that's an African value.

Parenting and honouring ancestors

... The next thing is take your parenting activities seriously. You know if each Black man would just simply support his own children - I'm not saying everybody else's children - just support your own child. ... If you support you own children then that would be a great help already within the Black community. Support your own children, take parenting seriously, and then in a spiritual sense, honour the ancestors - always honour the ancestors. Give your own children examples of their ancestors - name the ancestors. All religion is nothing more than the deification of ancestors. ... If you're not deifying your own ancestors you're deifying or making sacred somebody else's ancestors. Make your own ancestors sacred - do that for your children. Create ceremonies and initiations. ... If you do this you can also create rites of passage programmes for young children, particularly our male children. Our male children need rites of passage programming. This means that you give them historical, cultural and economic information exercises. ... [When they have learnt the information] ... at a certain period give them a public presentation, ... or publicly present them as having achieved certain information, and having come to a certain place. If you do this, what this creates for you is an opportunity for children then to pass this on, and we know that there are certain kinds of values that African descended children ought to have. Take that information and use that information to also move the community along - but fundamentally as Black men the protocols of institution building even at a small level, even beginning with study groups of five and six people in our home, this is the beginning process. ... If you do that I guarantee you that the future would be far brighter than anything we have known in the past.

Questions

• *Core values that separate African people from other people*
I think all people probably share similar values - I think that what is different may very well be what we emphasise. We emphasise different things. I'll tell you what we have said. We have developed a core list of values based on the classical African traditions that

20

we see in African cultures that ... are based on the principles of MA'AT. ... Fundamentally, ... what you have are values such as harmony, balance, order, justice, a sense of righteousness, a sense of truth, [and] a sense of reciprocity. These are the fundamental African values. ... It is rare that you see any statement in African traditions about pride. There's no value in the sense of pride - there is of course a sense of nobility in Africa. But we also say in a contemporary sense that in the African family in terms of African values in the US, ... principles such as courtesy, generosity, rhythm with nature and with other humans - that these are core values that we exhibit. There's no strong value at least I haven't seen it in the African culture for some notion of individual brief or something like that, I mean there are people in the community like that, but that is not a value of Africa.

- *Individual versus collective energies for practical initiatives*
Malcolm [X] used to say: 'when we try to think individually we can't do anything' - but look at this room - in this room if we think collectively, ... even five pounds per month, we can have our own place - but we just have to think collectively, ... start small at first. Because so long as we believe we can only be dependant and we don't wanna put [in] our own private money, and our own private energy into something, we can't do it, we will never do it. The only way we do it is to make a commitment - you make a commitment to your community. There are many examples here. I've read about examples that happen right here in the UK where some people have done this, and so I know it's possible, but I think that's how we have to do it.

... I know in the States ... people have built schools. ... You [might] only have ten students, but you can start a school, you can start a church. ... In the States we have one hundred colleges that African people started years ago, and most of those colleges are still in existence. Some of them are relatively small - I went to one [of them] ... for the first two years of my college experience. I went to a Black college [with] two hundred, three hundred students. ... It was a college that a Black man had started - Black people can do that - we can create institutions. Then of course you get institutions that are much larger, like Howard University, Texas Southern and Tuskegee. ... People just simply say: 'no, I'm gonna do this - I'm gonna take a group of students and we're gonna do this, we're gonna find them brothers, and we're gonna build this'. [This is similar to building] some houses for people like Claude [Hendrickson] did - there's all kinds - you can do this kind of thing.

- *Male organisations in the USA*
There are many - there is one I wanted to bring information about, the 'Mad Dad' programme, which is operated in the state of Florida. ... There are a number of parenting organisations [in the USA, and] ... a Black parenting magazine. ... There are many organisations and many institutions like that.

- *Internet use to create national and international networks*
I think it's a excellent idea - you should have my website, which is *Asante. net,* because on the website you will also find linkages to other Afrocentric individuals and institutions. ... [There] is also a *Net Noire,* which is a wonderful group of African people involved - [and] a directory that's coming out in Atlanta Georgia, of Black linkages. I can be in touch with the people in this organisation and get that information to you, but it means we have to have a passion for technology and be at the forefront of it as we have always been in the States. If you go to many universities in the US the main people who run the computers are often Africans.

- *Self-identity of African people using colour*
No, I think its very problematic, because first of all there is no geography that one can identify like that, and there are Black people almost in every continent. I think that it is wisest to have identification that is based essentially on either three things One, continent of original origin as far as you know [two], nationality or [three], language. ... There are a lot of people I know who have a problem saying that they are African, I've never had any problem saying that I was born in Georgia in the US - I knew

precisely that I was not a European, and I recognised that very early. I think these are the things that we have to overcome - we all come from that origin. I am an African man.

I am sorry that I don't have a chance to speak to you for two hours but we'll do it another time [See Molefi, 1998; Molefi and Abarry (eds.), 1994; Hilliard, 1996; Madhubuti, 1990].

Claude Hendrickson

He is the Head of Community Development at Lambeth College in London, [and] he's a freelance Education Consultant. I've heard him speak at a few conferences regarding males and Black boys in education, ... so let me introduce him - Trevor Gordon.

The first thing I want to say as usual is, it is good to be here - it's good to be in Leeds - it is good to be preaching to what I can see are the converted. It's always the same things, the same people, the same faces, the same level of commitment. [But] there [is also] ... a lot of faces in here I haven't seen before. If I had my full forty-five minutes I would acknowledge you all individually, because I think that's what being men together is about. It's about acknowledging all of us and all the work we do, not just me up on the stage, and I'm certain the Doctor would agree. It's about acknowledging the brother such as Jabari [Ta Seti] - it's about acknowledging the work that Paul [Obinna] does. It's about acknowledging my brothers from Huddersfield, ... that is what the coming together is all about. But I do feel like I'm gonna preach to the converted today - nevertheless let us do what we have to do.

... Putting my stuff together I thought I gotta squeeze two hours into forty-five minutes - [but now] I got forty-five minutes into half an hour. First thing I want to say as Black men is: 'the biggest problem that we've got is our timing'. We got to get it together. We should be listening to this brother [Molefi] for two hours - and there's no excuse - it just doesn't exist.

... I'm gonna to stick very much to the main focus that St. Clair [Brown] asked me to deal with today, ... the formation of a co-ordinating body for male forums across the UK. ... There are other meetings of Black men taking place today in Sheffield [and] London, ... [therefore] it is important that we begin to put together a national framework [of Black male forums]. ... This stuff is going on all over the country.

A bow to past organisations

I was asked to talk about Black male organisations from a historical, present pro-active community point of view - and I did a bit of research before, and basically it's a very difficult area to look into. There are very few men only organisations in the United

24

Kingdom, ... the few that have existed, have only existed for [the past] fifty years, ... [although] we've been here for three hundred [years] in terms of mass arrival in this country. ... However, just from a historical basis, the longest and most established all men's, all Black men's, or men of African origin in the United Kingdom, is the West Indian Service Men's Club that was formed just after World War Two (Circa 1946), by commonwealth ex-servicemen. I suppose all of us at some stage have heard about this particular organisation. I don't want to talk much about it, but in terms of its historical base, it is the oldest and most established men only organisation in the United Kingdom.

Moving on from that - I remember speaking to my father and my uncle about the Pan African Congress, ... (they were also influential in the sixties and the seventies), though not exclusively for men, ... many of my father's generation attended the meetings and the rallies in London, of the UK element of that particular movement. ... I'm certain that Dr. Asante similarly remembers. However, following the mysterious death of the main leader in London, the group tended to filter out. ... [We] tend to forget that many of our leaders who were outspoken, such as Franz Fanon, did vanish mysteriously about the same time - pushed out of windows. We need to remember that many of our people have mysteriously gone amiss in the past, and we need to give homage to the work that they did. Anyway, after this founder disappeared - I remember sitting down with my father, and my father telling me that things just disintegrated - so the Europeans who took him out knew what they were doing.

Building African male organisations
More recently there are many organisations that are enabling and assisting men of African origin, though very few have a men only brief. There is a great difficulty in developing men only organisations - and very briefly, I'm gonna tell you why. There are six keys points as far as I am concerned, and all of those of you who have heard me speak before know I do not mince my words - know what I do not wrap up - and know that I'm gonna deal with the issue.

I was rather looking forward today to coming up here and really dealing with some of the brothers, but as I say, I'm dealing with the converted. I was really hoping that I was gonna get some of the real brothers from Chapeltown in here today, and I could say: 'I don't care if you like me - I don't care what you think about me - I don't care what your opinions are of me, but hear me - I'm a messenger'. I was gonna deal with them because they need dealing with - but I'm in a hall now preaching to the converted. I'm gonna stick to that theme - I'm gonna run through and let you know why we have problems, and why there are difficulties around African men only organisations. Whether you agree with any of it or not really isn't the issue - the fact of the matter is the truth can hurt, but if you take it on-board it will set you free.

1. Male organisations require men
Reason number one is that to have a man only organisation takes men. ... I'm being serious, ... that is the most serious reason it takes to have a man only organisation. ... I travel nationally ... [and can see] that there is a lack of men out there - a lack of men coming to the community organisations - a lack of men coming into the schools - a lack of men getting themselves involved. ... [Therefore], if we are gonna have men only organisations, we need men, and I'm not patronising anybody. I travel up and down the country, I go to the seminars, I'm on the circuit, and all I see are the sisters. The sisters are getting up out of their beds on a Saturday, ... the sisters are bringing along the children, and the children are mixing and mingling in the corner, and the sisters are doing the work. What's wrong with us - what's wrong with the brothers? If I go to the 'blues' on a Saturday, I find the brothers - if I go to a pub in the evening, I can find the brothers - if I go to the betting shop in the daytime, I can find the brothers. I'll tell you something else - even in Sainsbury's I can't find the brothers. However, the only brothers you find in Sainsbury's are the single brothers - because when you're a single brother it's no problem to go down Sainsbury's because you might find a nice girl. Yeah, but the minute you got a wife and children you don't bother go Sainsbury's again. It's the truth - I'm gonna deal with it today - this is the truth.

I want to draw your attention to Carl [Hylton] who produced a wonderful booklet last year and deserves to be acknowledged for it. Carl says ... [that]: 'women have a high participation in African-Caribbean groups and organisations that are at the forefront of maintaining and rebuilding African cultural identities' [Hylton (ed.), 1997a]. Women - the sisters - they're the ones doing it - they're the ones who ring me up in my home - they're the ones who are constantly on the phone. There are some days when I find it difficult not to feel ashamed to be a man of African origin. We're letting ourselves down badly - very, very, badly. It takes men to have a men only organisation - so we need to remember that.

As I said, I'm preaching to the converted because a lot of the faces I see in here are the brothers who come out, and the brothers who do the work - they are the brothers who go into school. Why don't we go into school? ... What's going on? Every time I'm up in the school and there's somebody from the African community in the teacher's face, it's a sister - the brothers don't go near the education establishments. I'm gonna tell you the problem I have with some of this as well - the mind-set it leaves white people with. ... You want to know why they have messed with you as Black men? I work in these places - I sit in the tearoom with my white colleagues - I listen to the comments that they pass about us as Black men. It makes me want to go to the toilet and lock the door. It's no good because you don't want to get up and go to school, - no, because my baby mother can deal with the school. Why does she do it - why aren't you visible up there as well? That's why they're gonna mess with your sons, and keep messing with your sons until you get up and go up there and show them that you're visible - that they can't be getting away with this - we've got to change - we've got to change.

2. Lack of self-awareness
Issue number two - lack of self-awareness that leads to self-development, ... and we have the ideal man here today who should have been given two hours to deal with the self-development [issues]. Yes: who am I? What am I? Why am I? I

want you all to go home today, and if you can't answer those three questions, you got serious problems. ... You can't move on - you can't join an all Black men's network, and you can't develop your community and contribute to it.

[Here are the answers] very quickly. Who am I? This is your past - what you are, and your ancestors where they originally came from. How did they live, what sort of people were they, and what did they create, build and accomplish.

What am I? Your initial answer to this should be: 'a person of African origin'. You have the longest and greatest history of all people on earth - you were the first people on earth. You are the equal of your opposite gender - equal. You're not greater than the sisters, you're equal to the sister. That's another issue the brothers need to deal with. Yeah - two halves make a whole - you're half of it - you're not the whole of it. You have great intelligence without which your ancestors could not have invented science, medicine, chemistry, physics, mathematics and psychology. You are the physical reincarnation of the one universal God. You wanna know what God looks like? Look in the mirror. Once you begin to grasp the concept of what you are, and this being understood and accepted, it logically leads to you asking the next question: 'why am I'?

[Why am I]? I am special - I am to live in peace with my fellow man and respect and protect mother earth. I have won the lottery of life. One in a million sperm get fertilised, so you're special, and therefore I must appreciate and value my existence and specialness. I must try and live with the attitude of the God that created me. I must protect the young and assist in their development, bearing in mind that they are the future. I must love life and this includes love myself for what I am. Community involvement begins with fellowship - fellowship is natural to the African way of life - [natural for] African men. It is a natural part of the cycle of African men to come together in the village ... to take fellowship. There is a hierarchy - I'm not telling you that

28

there isn't, but it's not hierarchy as you see from the European perspective - this is something that is natural. This is how African men have developed for thousands of years, if not hundreds of thousands of years, through the coming together in the village to determine the future of the village. Do you follow where I'm coming from? You come into this European society, and me better than you - you better than me - you understand what I'm saying? ... Black men's organisations - organisation of men of African origin - it's natural to us - it's not foreign.

3. Class and caste

Issue number three that stops us is the class or the caste system. I was in Manchester last week with my brother Paul [Obinna], and spent the weekend with him. I take fellowship with my brothers - I got no problem about getting on the train and going and taking fellowship with my fellow African man, because that's how I'm gonna develop - that's how I make my contribution. I was taking fellowship last weekend and we were speaking about class and caste. ... Caste, colour, class ... is the one subtle difference to us [compared to] ... the American system - there's a very subtle class, caste system in play in this country - and what is it doing? It's developing into something where you have a group of what they call middle class Blacks - you hear me - middle class Blacks - and it's all about capitalism, materialism money and wealth. Middle class Blacks on the move. ... A survey published in the *New Nation* ... [states that] significant proportions of young Blacks have joined the Saab, skiing and sun dried tomatoes brigade. They are the avant-garde of the new emerging middle class. The survey says that 44% of people aged between 18 and 35 categorise themselves as middle class, ... and a third describe themselves as Black British [See Sunday Times, 1996, 9]. I have a real problem - the question that the brother raised about the term 'Black' - I've been raising that. I used to get lynched by my own [people for using that term], ... so I'm really pleased to see that we're coming around now, because I'm still looking around for this country called 'Black'.

Now things have changed - the BMW is still the status symbol in our community, but kids are meeting people who have BMW's and earned them from working in a computer company rather than by hustling on the street. My word - serious thing. I just want to read [this quote from the Sunday Times about] ... Jennifer Fox, IT Consultant, who lives in an all white village, in a nice little barn cottage ... with a nice middle class husband:

'People always ask me how I've done it - the answer is I work hard. I started as a sixteen-year-old single mother but I sat my exams while I was pregnant because I always knew that was the way out. I am middle class now and proud of what I have achieved, and others can do it too' (Sunday Times, 1996, 9).

Whose she fooling, apart from herself? [Here is another quote] - Sarah [Ebanja] is a manager:

'I have worked extremely hard but with hindsight I haven't had a difficult run up the ladder. Being Black is definitely a disadvantage sometimes, but it can also be a plus' [Sunday Times, 1996, 9].

How many of you can relate to this? 'The white establishment needed a few token Blacks around - I have fitted into this need'. Lord have mercy - and there's Trevor McDonald here. Trevor Phillips is about the only one whose basically (and you know there's times I disagree with Trevor) ... getting it right.

... [These are the issues that's] stopping us from getting together - this caste rubbish - this middle class rubbish, when a few of us feel real nice looking down on the rest. Do you follow me? It has got to stop. I'll tell you something - when I'm at home with my two children, and I'm down in the corner praying to my creator, you know the two most important things I ask for? Humbleness and humility. I beg him to control my ego, because as the first man of God I've got a big ego - and that's what I beg my creator ... [to control] everyday. Because Trevor Gordon gets called to do this - Trevor Gordon gets called to do that - Trevor Gordon can stand in front of people, stroke his ego, and feel nice about himself. Let me tell you my brothers, behind closed doors that's the one thing I beg my creator to do is to keep that under control because that's mashing us up.

We've got to finish this class thing - it's a very British thing. I just want to bring your attention to ... a piece of work by a guy called Homi Bhabha [1986] - he's a writer. He wrote a piece of work called *Of Mimicry and Man* - he's a South East Asian brother, but it's a wonderful piece of work. Let me tell you what Homi Bhabha wrote. He writes about the European who sees us in suits, and you're a nigger in a suit - he sees you in a Porsche, and you're a nigger in a Porsche - he sees you with a five bed-roomed house, and you're a nigger with a five bed-roomed house. I don't know where half of these middle and upper class Blacks are getting off from, ... because they could be dirt poor white people, but no matter how much wealth you've got, you're a nigger with your wealth. Homi Bhabha articulates that particular mind-set so well - do you follow me? We need to understand we can have the money, we can have the wealth, but a lot of white people still see you as a nigger. Eddie Murphy had a revelation when a dirt farmer spat on his Ferrari when he was driving through Hollywood, and that's when Eddie got Black and did the video, and wore the African gowns. He's got fifteen Black cars - and when the dirt farmer spat on his Ferrari, Eddie leaned over and asked him what did you do that for - he said: 'you're just a nigger in a Ferrari' - you follow me? Let's move on.

4. <u>Bad attitude towards other Africans</u>
Linked to that number three, another reasons we can't move on is the attitude towards each other. There is no group of men on the face of the planet who bad mouth each other, put down each other, and get on top of each other like us. It sucks - it's a real bad attitude - do you get me? [For example] - bouy, that Trevor Gordon, he can chat, man - and: 'how come he ain't changed his name to an African name? How come he ain't wearing an African gown'? ... Everybody wants to find an excuse to put down on us - we are envious of each other and jealous of each other. We

don't see each other doing stuff and say: 'I wish you well'. We don't see each other having nice things and say: 'bouy, I'm gonna get mine'. No, you want mine - you understand what I'm saying? It's time to talk the truth man - we got a real attitude about how we see each other, and some of that's coming out of slavery, some of that is what they did to us, but it's time to realise yourself, remember what I told you - who, what and why.

We gotta stop bad mouthing each other, and putting down on each other. ... [Saying for example] - 'who does brother Paul [Obinna] think he is, because he's organised a whole heap of conferences in Manchester, who does he think he is? Who does the brother here [Nat Lindo] think he is because he's doing all the work in Huddersfield? ... If I pulled up today in a Ferrari do you know how many people would badmouth me - oh yeah? Trevor Gordon talks about Black history but he has a big Ferrari though. Oh man, I'm fed up of it. That's why we can't come together as Black men. Yet we all start from the same standpoint, there's very little difference between us in this room. ... Most of us coming out of working class parents, and most of us coming out of the same kind of stock. [But] people look at me and say it's aright for you Trev - yeah, look at you - you're educated. ... Until the age of thirty I didn't have an education to my name - I used to sell weed - I used to be called a gangster - I used to be into sound systems. ... Listen, if I end up with a Ferrari nobody can tell me I don't deserve it, because unnu have the same chance as me, because unnu come out of the same background as me - there's no difference between us. How many of us in here have got upper class parents who sent us to public school - put your hands up? [No hands were raised] So don't put down on me - you understand where I'm coming from? So start taking responsibility for your own actions. Where do you think it started from with me? It started with evening classes, ... with rain pissing down on my head, freezing cold dirty buses, lecturers who didn't want to help me go through. You think I had an easy walk? Then people want to look at me and say: 'it's aright for you'.

- *Child rearing - fear and respect*

[I talked with] ... brothers Paul [Obinna] and Andy [Forbes] ... about this - the lack of respect we've got for each other, and this line between fear and respect. ... We ain't got no respect for each other - that's the bottom line - you know why? Because we're growing up to not have any. You see me, I respect my fellow African, ... you know why? Because I had a father who brought me up to respect. I used to get my arse ripped for non-respect - ripped off. ... [Now] I've got fifteen and sixteen year olds in my college, in my face - the next generation, in my face. When I was a young boy I used to go to dances at fifteen and sixteen - and I go in the dance, and I'll be looking for my father's friends because they would kick my arse if they saw me. That was respect - and do you think I could go back to my father and say Dad your friends ... kicked my arse? He would kick it again. You got a whole heap of Europeans out there telling us we mustn't beat our children - you mustn't do that to them. Pick up your Bible if you want to know what you should be doing to your children, or if you're in the Nation, pick up the Quran. It does not say we should not deal with our children firmly. I got a big problem - a lot of my white colleagues don't like my teaching style - you know why? Because a whole heap of the African youths in my college, when they walk down the corridor [and they see me, it's] hello Trevor, hello Mr. Gordon. Respect - they give me respect, ... you know why? Because I will kick their arse if they don't, and they're going to grow up being good rounded men of African origin because of it.

The Times Educational Supplement ring me up: 'teaching style is a sensitive issue - Black teaching style is a sensitive issue'. ... They ask me what I thought. [They said]: 'we know strong discipline works with Black kids'. ... I ... am frequently told that I'm hard. I find it insulting to be told how to handle children [they are not 'kids'] from my own 'race', especially when I see them responding and learning. ... Whose responsible for the Black men out there - the young ones - whose responsible for them? We are. ... So when you are sixty or seventy and they're coming up and kicking away your walking stick, and they're dissing you - and they buss your head - and they're troubling your daughters - who you gonna blame? ... I got four daughters, and let me tell you I ain't gonna be blaming nobody - yes, fear and respect - you show me the division. I learnt respect through fear, and it ain't done me no harm whatsoever.

5. Respect for all women

You notice I use the term 'all' women - I mean white women too. All women deserve to be treated with dignity and respect irrespective of their colour. I don't have a problem with cross-cultural relationships; I do have a problem however, if it causes Black men in particular to forgo their cultural heritage.

Just remember the culture, and remember that all women deserve respect. There's a natural affinity between men and women of different cultural origins, and this is articulated in Bradley [1991], *The Ice Man Inheritance.*

[What I'm going to say very quickly, is based on the 'reflection'] work that Paul Obinna does ... around brothers and sisters - around the gender relationship concerning how we are disrespecting 'our' women on a regular full time basis. Men tend to find security in power, career, skills, information, intelligence, women and physical strength. Women tend to find security in family, a strong mate, sharing, communication, their own emotions and being loved. We've got to begin to understand why it is that we are not getting along with the sisters. I got a wife - I've been with her for nineteen years. Believe me - me and her kick-off on a regular basis, but I don't go packing my bags, and I don't go screwing out - you follow where I'm coming from? If I do decide to screw out, she ain't gonna find out. I'm dealing with the issue today, because Black man seem to think that everybody have to know - that's another problem we got - this big ego. We down the road with Susie - why? White people do it but they keep it to themselves. The Asian community do it - nobody screwing out like them - but they keep it to themselves. We do it, everybody

34

have to know - Sharon, Linda, Susie - why? Even if you can't be faithful to one woman hold it down because it looks bad, it's making it look bad for us as a people.

6. Fatherhood and family responsibilities

... This is another thing that is stopping us from coming together as men, yeah, because slavery did something to us in relation to the family. We got a serious problem about making a commitment to our children - we got a serious problem about making a family commitment. I'm not saying that relationships don't break up - yes they do. [For example] my first daughter's mother, ... [we could not get on, but I supported by daughter]. Every weekend [a month] come hell [or high water] ... I ... paid maintenance by Bank Standing Order, [for] eighteen years. I look at my [present] wife now and I [can remember that we] went without. [She use to ask]: ... 'what are you doing'? I said: 'I have to take this money down the road for Sharlene'. She said: 'we're broke'. I said: 'yes, but I have to take this money down the road for Sharlene'. Do you understand where I'm coming from? Because no women is going to look at me as a man and tell me about what I didn't do from what I do. I praise the creator that my daughter is in university now. I didn't grow her - she didn't live with me everyday, but I was there for her.

What is the African family? It's an extended family system. It is a correct model upon which to develop our children. The European nuclear family is firstly the product of environment - and again Bradley *The Ice Man Inheritance*, [gives a good overview of this]. ... Secondly, [the European nuclear family was created because of] capitalism, and the need for landowners to control the bulk of the peasant population of the United Kingdom. That's what it's about. It is a European individualistic approach, and there is a primary requirement for capitalism within that process, where most of the benefits of wealth go to those who already have wealth and power. Yet how can we sustain the extended or African family culture when we cannot see the benefit of that broader system of care? If we don't change, all of us in here are gonna end up in a old peoples home - you know why? Because that's the culture - that is the European ... culture that they're gonna put in us. ... [But] my daughters ain't gonna put me in no old aged peoples home - trust me. But some of you are heading there. ... When you're in there reflecting back on your life and asking how did my sorry Black arse end in this place just remember what Trevor Gordon told you today.

We must begin to revive the extended family and the way it was used for fifty thousand years. I'm gonna go home tonight - there's a whole barrel load of children in my house. I'm gotta be going in my front room and locking the door - my daughters have invited this one here to sleep, and that one there to sleep. Me look pon me wife and say: 'lord God', [and] ... play some music and chill out, because that is the extended African family network. ... When people that we know want to have a weekend off, they can bring their children and leave them with us, and if I want to go to Manchester for a weekend, my wife can take my children and leave them with some other brothers and sisters - that's how it works.

I gonna conclude. When we can get all of this together - when we can do what is natural to us - because everything that I've told you ... today is natural and some of it is about honesty. When we can do all of that - then we can move things forward.

Why do we need organisations for African men - because we need political power. We're only gonna get that through these organisations - new Labour - new racism. I got no time for this Labour Party - I've got no time for none of them - you understand me? I wanna sit down with the Conservatives - I wanna sit down with the Liberals - and I want to sit down with the Labour Party. I wanna do it with a mandate behind me of three million people of African origin in this country, and I wanna say: 'whose gonna give me' - and I don't care cause I'll go back [to the community] and say vote. If I come and say Trevor Gordon says vote Conservative - vote Conservative - and if I say vote Liberal - vote

Liberal. If I say vote Labour - then vote Labour, because whoever I tell you to vote for are gonna give us something. Eighty-three percentage of African-Caribbeans in this country vote for the Labour party. Forty-four percentage of white people vote for them, and they're shiting all over us. We need Black men's organisation to control that vote, and I'm more than willing to sit down with Mr Haigh - sit down with Mr Blair, and say: 'what have you done for me lately'? Which is what the Jews do - which is what the South East Asians do - and they go off and they vote en-mass. All I want is five things. They're in power for five years - gimme five things. I want five schools for our children in five of our major conurbations - I want five institutes to deal with the mentally ill. ... I want five of everything, and then I want twenty-five million pounds on top of it too - and I don't care who gives it to me. See where I'm coming from? To shift it from socialism and the Labour Party, because they're taking the piss out of you more than the Tories are.

Economic power that's another thing you gotta do. We got to work with each other, but that comes through the trust. I got my own company - I'm setting up another company with two brothers down here. We met at the weekend, and we're gonna set up a company. ... Let me tell you how this company's gonna work. If I go out and earn a thousand pounds, and Paul [Obinna] goes out the same week and earns two thousand pounds, and Andy [Forbes] goes out the following week and earns three thousand pounds - we're not gonna sit down there and say: 'but me earn more than you, so me fi get more than you, and me a do all the work, and you not doing it'. ... We've decided that we're gonna rise above all that stuff, and that we're all gonna work as hard as we can. Whatever's in the kitty at the end of the day, is in the kitty at the end of the day. Whoever needs to draw from it - draws from it. We're not get into, because I did 'X', I must draw 'Y'. ... That's what stops the development of the Black economy - talk to your South East Asian colleagues about that, because they're not all pulling their weight equally, but yet look how they split the proceeds.

Respect for the African family, and that starts with respecting yourself - respect for our elders - and that comes with fear and discipline. Education - it's got to become trendy for our young men to want to get educated - like how it's trendy for them to wear them trousers round them batty - like it's trendy for them to go out and curse bad word. ... You see me, I've trained my daughters [to] chase the boys who are going to school - chase the boys who are getting educated. ... You could have the biggest beama, the most jewellery, the slickest lyrics - but you ain't in school or college getting educated - my daughters ain't coming near you.

... [We need to] isolate those of us who are going to carry us down. I'm willing to do it - these middle class do goody nastiness' who are carrying us down - who stroke their ego looking down. If they ain't got some Black people to look down on they don't look good. [They seem to be saying]: 'but look at me - I educated myself, and I raised above [it], ... I'm middle class now. I just know the other people down there could do it if they really tried'. [The people carrying us down], ... they've got to be isolated, and they've got to be cut off. ... Trevor don't name no names, [but] it's time to start naming names. ... But one person can't do it, because one person will get hurt - but a men's organisation can do that, because where there's an organisation they can't pick on one person. We got certain people out there in our community making a lot of money, and they're doing nothing for us. We need to name names - and that's another reason why we need an organisation of Black men, men of African origin.

I'm gonna wind-up here. I hope you found what I had to say valuable. I'm sorry that the right sort of brothers weren't here necessarily to hear the message. All I can say from the bottom of my heart is: brothers we got to change - we gotta change now you know [that] ... Europeans are coming in - Armenians are coming in - Yugoslavs are coming in. If you think we can sit here for another twenty years waiting to take economic advantage, forget it because the time is not infinite. If we as men of African origin don't move within the next five years, pack unnu bag and leave - you hear me? We got to get it together because there are other immigrant communities coming in the country en-mass now - you follow me? They're gonna take the riches that we should be getting. ... All of a sudden we're gonna wake up one morning in the year 2004 and say: 'shit'! We gotta do it now. Thank you.

Where are we now - Black men's forum organisations

Marimba played by - **Musa Suma**

| Performing artist | **Patrice Naiambana** | Royal Shakespeare Company |

It is very good to be here and see you all. What is even more amazing is to see Black faces. After being in this country for eighteen months, and to see no white faces - it is of great health to my bones. Thank you very much for having me. Do you all know who I am? ... My name is General Alfred Providence Mukata. I come from Komera [in Africa]. I have been variously described as a bafoon - an arsehole - a dictator - a good father - a king - a ruler. I have been called all manner of names. When you look at who is calling the name, then you can decide whether it is true, whether I deserve those names. I have ruled Komera for eight years. It is a wonderful country - very, very rich in diamonds, gold, semi-precious stones, oil, sea, stars, and very beautiful women.

The reason why I am in this country, is because I refused to allow the British to get at my copper reserves. I have been called a dictator. The reason I have been called a dictator is because I refused their demands. In this world you have to give and take sometimes. But they were taking too much. I put my foot down and all of a sudden I am a dictator.

My people love me - most of them. The ones who are not in cahoots are with the foreign imperial masters. But as life would have it, you have to fight fire with fire sometimes, because of that they call me a dictator. So I decided to look in the dictionary to find out what is a dictator. The dictionary tells me that a dictator is a ruler who is effectively not constrained by constitution. This means that if the constitution that you had in the past, in the days of old - if those constitutions and traditions or ways of ruling ourselves, have been eradicated - that means there are no constitutions any longer. We have to develop one. So therefore you have to rule. They call these persons a dictator. This is fine by me. If you are in your home, and you have wife and children, and you do not lay down the law, there will be chaos. Somebody has to say this is this.

Because I refused the British their ways in my country, they financed a coup against me. I could no longer get hold of the millions that I had put away for a rainy day. ... You see, if you want to rule in Africa and you do not have millions, you are finished. There are always thieves and gangsters hanging around, ready to usurp your position. You have to be able to finance counter-coup. You have to be ready for the Palestinians that will be coming this way - the Americans who will be coming that way - the very Black brother that you may have grown up with - you have to be ready for him. The children are coming up, and somebody has to be providing, looking out for them - that is the constant struggle in Africa today. I do not want to go into the dynamics of dictatorship right now, but I thought somehow I should introduce myself on that political level, because that is why I am here.

Now I have no Mercedes Benz, I have no drivers. I have been stripped - but one thing I have not been stripped of is the dignity and beauty that God breathed into me from my mother's breast. I have not been stripped of that. She breathed into me a sense of justice and respect - I have not been stripped of that. I stand here today, in exile - but like you, I have not been stripped of fire to stand for what is right, and I will not be stripped. ... I proceed in exile ... [with the] armour of righteousness.

So they gave me two white people with an English BA, who the Foreign Office allocated ... to look after me. They are not always conducive to my own agenda. I find myself operating in another man's language - in another man's country - in another man's ways and means. That I think gives you cause for reflection. So, I began to reflect - I said: 'Alfred, what have you done to end up in this situation, when the British Foreign Minister is asking me why are you going to a conference where no white people are - is that not undemocratic and racist'? I said to him: 'when a dog farts a lot, dog will like his own fart'. He asked me to explain, I asked him if he wanted me to fart? He soon got the message. They have continually been undemocratic and racist to the point where they cannot even define racism for themselves, ... so that even if they wanted to, they cannot solve the problem. I believe, divinely, we are in this situation for a reason - nothing happens for nothing. ... We are here to civilise this country through our suffering and our experiences. Bishop had to let me come, because I said: 'I don't want the bodyguards, I don't want your MI5 - keep them - because I know you probably have microphone in this place anyway'. That's aright, no problem - truth will always win - but let's uncover the truth. I said: 'I'm coming' - I came.

I came off the train, - a very humbling experience. I had to use the train - normally, I have a Mercedes to take me where I am going. But it taught me something because I had to pass through W. H. Smith at the train station, and I was looking at all the pictures - all of them with women with their breasts hanging down. Everywhere you look, women's breasts hanging down. Look there - groin open. Look there - she is opening her mouth as if to put something inside. I began to ask myself: 'what type of people are these'? They say I can't speak English very well - I don't care whether I can speak English very well. I said: 'what type of people are these'? - and it came to me that they must be mad. If you cannot respect the woman who gave life to you, and you have to put her image everywhere with her legs open and her bottom sticking out, and her mouth open - that means you don't respect where you came from, just in terms of the biological sense. Then when I saw the title of this conference, *Social Exclusion*, I said: 'I don't mind being socially excluded from mad people, I don't mind. I am very happy to be excluded from the madness of sexual immorality'. ... [Are there] positive aspects of being excluded? When life throws you lemons - make lemonade.

... I was reading a paper about the Falklands. ... I want to read ... to you one article that I saw today:

'Shortly before the Second World War, Neville Chamberlain's government commissioned a secret report, which still remains classified to this day. ... The conclusions of the report devastatingly reveal that Britain had no chance for winning it's case for ownership of the Falklands in an independent, international, judicial tribunal, given our history (that's the white man talking about his own history, for a change), of piracy and aggression against Argentina, which was the only basis for our occupation of the Islands' [Livingstone, 1998].

Does that sound familiar? The report showed that the first settlement on the island was by France in 1764, but after protest from Spain, France handed it back over to the Spanish, receiving compensation for doing so. Almost immediately Britain established a small settlement on the main western island, but she was rapidly expelled by Spanish action in 1770. In the negotiations that followed, Spain allowed Britain to return in exchange for a secret (that word, again), undertaking that Britain would quietly withdraw once the dispute was no longer in the public eye - an undertaking that was honoured by British withdrawal in 1774 [Livingstone, 1998].

(I don't want to waste your time, but the word secret has appeared twice). If you have to be doing things in secret, plenty, plenty, plenty - you are a liar. You are stepping into the arena of lying - you are a liar. Why do you have to be doing things in secret all the time if what you are doing is aright, if it is OK? That's the second thing I discovered about these people, although I knew it all along. When I came to this country, when you are in a different situation you see things differently. They are not only mad - they are liars.

Here is the main point I am coming to. ... In 1776, they transferred the administration of the Falkland Islands to Buenos Aires, and following the Declaration of Independence in 1816, Argentina appointed the Governor of the islands, who continued in control until 1832 - until Britain invaded and expelled the local Argentinean occupation. Until that time, until the present day, Argentina understandably has never accepted Britain's seizure of the islands [Livingstone, 1998]. I said to myself: 'this is remarkably familiar to me somehow'. It suggests to me that they have never changed - and when a leopard refuses to change its spots, don't keep looking for it to change.

You all know I am preaching to the converted. Where I come from, there has not been that much exposure of our own expression, I need to just recap a little bit, so you know where I am coming from. Of course, these facts were not relayed to the British people, either by the parliamentary opposition to Mrs Thatcher - a British dictator - or by the mass media. Indeed, even Britain's, political moves towards Argentina shortly before the war were rapidly airbrushed from the records. If a British man can talk about his own history like that, what can he say about our own situation here - and I am talking about the present day.

The past has been very well documented, and I don't need to come and tell you about the past - and it's an extremely important past. You see the land of Africa, if we don't own it - we - when I say: 'we' - I mean everybody here. If we cannot lay claim to the land - I am not talking about it's regimes or the things that are going wrong - [the things] that are negative - because that is happening everywhere. Let him who is without sin, let him cast the first stone. What I am talking about is the physical land. Everybody wants a piece of Africa. Africa is not for everybody to have - it is for us. Whether you go over there physically, or you stay here - you have to go back. We own here too. We bought it, we paid for it, we sacrifice for it. It is ours - our ancestors died for it - so we do not have to go anywhere - it is ours.

Two weeks ago when I got the call from the brothers to come, I said: ... 'I am very interested to meet some Black people, because I am Black - more than that - I am an African'. I was in the laundry having to do something I have never done before - I was putting my money in. I saw a chap with some high dreadlocks. He needed a light for a cigarette. There was a Nigerian fella sitting next to him. The Nigerian man said: 'here is the light'. He say he didn't want. Then another fella came in and they were talking, you know the way they talk: 'wha guan'? He light the cigarette. I asked myself why? I asked him, I said: 'my brother'. He said: 'I am not his brother'. I said: 'friend'. He said: 'I am not his friend'. I said: 'my man' - I tried to touch like I see them do. I asked him why did you not accept a light from that other brother? He said to me: 'mind your own business man'. I am not used to being talked to like that. I am not used to those situations, and I did not know what to do. I said: 'why'? He said: 'just come out from my face you bobo man'. I spoke to the Nigerian man and asked what is bobo - he explained. I said: 'ha, ha - a man calling me bobo - he is Black, and Black is calling me names'. Is there something going on that I do not understand? ... I was confused. ... I went home and was really puzzled. There was no point in asking the MI5 people. I was very very confused. ... I was most puzzled, and I thought this must be one of the consequences of divide and rule.

... When I was reinstated as leader of Kumeria, I had just come out of Sandhurst. When you come out of Sandhurst they get all the people who they feel they can work with - those who were on time and very punctual. They take you all to a secret conference where they show you how to stash money. They take us there and teach us about all kinds of things. Then they tell us where to buy bombs. Most of us we try to play the game, thinking that we will get what we want - then when we get back we will be able to do our own thing. Except it was a trap. When we get there, and when you think you pick this one, or that one to be your cabinet minister, low and behold this one has been trained by CIA - this one has been trained by Russia.

They are all around you. You start to smell them, so you have to start getting rid of them one by one. Before you know it you are doing things you never made up your mind to ever do. You are trapped. Because I cannot allow stench in my house I have to get rid of him - of course, after all, he might poison everything. Once you do that you cannot stop. That is what happens when you shed blood. Before you know it you are trapped by your good intentions.

... Some of us say I cannot do anything - I will just steal the country ... once I feed my family and my fifteen wives and some other people. ... Those who ... are not really in the right place in the first place ... found themselves there - [where] temptation got too strong. If you see the wealth in my country. I wonder if anybody has that moral rectitude. When wealth is put in front of you in the quantities that it is back home, whether any of you [could resist it]. It is a very passionate thing. I am not trying to accuse anyone. ... Is there anybody here who has never been tempted? [Someone answered yes] Then you do not have a conscience. If you do not have the conscience then you do not have the goal. If you do not have the goal you are working in darkness. If you working in darkness you cannot see. That means you lead other people into a pit of destruction.

Have you seen a woman, so fine, so beautiful, so gorgeous inside and outside - you do not want to eat it? You do not want to touch it. Have you ever met a women like that? You have? ... I have seen such a woman. Such a woman is Africa. It is difficult to understand. ... I have not had an opportunity to talk like this since I have been here. The images that you see of Africa, if you notice - do not reflect that. If you see Africa on the television it is animals, starving children, Oxfam posters with starving children with big bellies. So you are likely to think: 'what is happening over there - what is wrong with those people'? I can understand that when I sat down and looked for myself, and saw the images coming in day after day.

The positive images seem to be in the white or different colour to us. I thought that must be another form of deform, of divide and rule - deform by insinuation - deform by mental illness. If you are always seeing something that does not look like you, well it's bound [to have an effect on you]. The one that you see that looks like you has big stomach. The one that looks like you is only another problem. We have just seen [Falklands quote] one of their own talking about what happened, how they dictated - they invented dictatorship these ones.

... It is important for me to hold my brother's hand - whether I like him or not, I have to hold my brother, ... I have to hold your hand. If by force - I have to hold you - otherwise it would be so easy just to decimate everything. ... We all acknowledge, we know what to do - we all understand the goals, but we are walking in bitterness. We just want our own right to express ourselves, not to be any-body's dogs-body. That is a right - it is not anything to fight about. It is not anything to get into conflict or anything like that. It's a right to express yourself - tell your whole story - to love - to rear your children. The obstacles that are stopping us from doing that must be ruthlessly exposed and eradicated. Sometimes things stop us. It is a thing called unity - disunity. I notice that there are so many religions. I find that there are a lot of evangelistic fervour - energy - which is very good. At times it seems to deflect [and] confuse a lot of people. If what I believe in is true, then the fruits will follow. Actions always speak louder than words.

One day I am going to buy this building [West Yorkshire Playhouse] and then they cannot move us from room to room. I will buy this building and extend Chapeltown to surround me. I tell you the Africans do it. ... We back home, we need you, and you need us. The circle has to be somehow completed. I am sorry I have not been able to go into it, but one day - maybe. There are others here that are actually much more [capable] to stand and teach - support those people.

My final thing. When I was coming up I was writing this. When I look at you my sons, tears flow, because in you I see the salvation of Africa. I am not trying to put down wherever else you may be from, Brazil, or St Kitts. You see that land - it is ours - that land there is OURS. I do not need to fight a white man on his own ground and say give me this. When I have the land I can buy his land five million times over, if we educate ourselves into what that land can actually mean now. If we were to become politically literate when they putting their things on television, we should be able to say: 'LIE, LIE, LIE'. We should be able to do that, and your children should be able to go: 'yes it is lie'. So that is what is true. Like my elder was saying, he say: 'when we have these types of things [conferences] - the little ones should be with us. (They are not going to behave well - do not give them any yams or plantains). So they can see you are linking with one another - how you are talking. Then they will say: 'yes' - because of what they see - osmotic teaching, osmotic love'.

So you are the salvation of Africa. You are the seed of our ancestry. You are the living fruit of the despised, lacerated human beings who died on the high seas of slavery. But, out of their dying black lips they prayed their dignity, beauty strength and power into your unborn souls. How else do you think you survive? Whatever happen - I do not care what happen, you are standing here strong. You do not look like victims to me - you do not look like muggers to me. You are standing here each one of you - kings - strong. That is because when each one of those were going down, they were praying for the children. Tell you why, never underestimate the blessing or curse of a dying man. Life and death are in the power of the tongue. In some very strange way you are there. For me to look at you and deliberately have problem with you - or even if I do not understand you - if I do not want to listen to you, and you do not want to listen to me, then do not expect anybody anywhere to listen to you.

Claude Hendrickson

When they want to socially exclude us it's not for us to look into the negative aspects of this social exclusion, but to look into the positive things - because if we're socially excluded from them, that should make us unified by ourselves. Therefore, let's not stick under the negativity of social exclusion but look into the positive side of social exclusion.

In the next session there are supposed to be two options - to stay together in this room - and there was an option for a workshop for under twenty-one year olds. ... That was suggested ... [because] sometimes younger people find it hard to move with the word and the speaking of older people, and because they are not used to coming to this kind of things. So we get on with it, and they get lost in it. ... [Question] - do people want a small workshop environment, or we can stay as in this one room, and go with it as it is? ... [Answer] - stay in this one room.

... [Let's] move on and look at some positive things by groups in Britain. ... One of the main reasons for having this conference is to look into the development of some kind of foundation - some kind of co-ordinated meeting - some kind of national body. [The first group representative] I'm gonna go with [is] Chris Thomas from the Nubian Men's Group in Bradford. Each speaker has six minutes - but I'd like to say to the young people who are here that if at any time you are unsure of what is being said, stick you hand up. If you're confused, ask - don't ever be afraid to ask - the way to find out is by asking. This is about you, and about your future, so any of you younger people want information, don't be frightened.

Chris Thomas
Knowledge from struggle

I'm not prepared - I've just been thrown in at the deep end - but ... Nubian Men's Group, we're almost to our second year - we do an array of things. I'd like to just mention one thing - it was the Stephen Lawrence Enquiry. We had a banner - and we had a few things explaining the atrocities that went on, and are still going on - it's the tip of the iceberg. When we tried to get into the meeting ... three security guards decided to search all the Black males. There were three hundred people at the enquiry and they decided to search all the Black males. I was searched - the brother behind me objected - another brother allowed the person to search him, and they just for some unknown reason, they decided to manhandle him. He tried to explain to them that he didn't want to be roughed up, and all of a sudden the police appeared, TV cameras, press - just appeared literally from nowhere. I was stood in the foyer by myself - within seconds they were around us - there's a fracas, and it's in the papers - a picture of us there. The point I'm making is when we are in a struggle, when we are fighting we've got to be aware of everything. We had a knowledge that the enemy would do certain things - [but] even with our ... knowledge, we still got set up [because we were naive]. It made it clear to me every-body's against us.

We went to the Ten Thousand Man March, and the majority of people taking pictures were white people. We don't know where the pictures are, we don't know what they're gonna do with the pictures. I just think we should be very vigilant and keep on going. You might have seen [our report] in the newsletter - *Nubian News* - Nigel [Guy] will speak briefly about that - and that's all I've got to say.

Nigel Guy
Organisation building

We [Nubian Men's Group] came about through one of our brothers in Bradford, who had an urge that the youths were not talking to (what the establishment classed us as), older men. What I define as the youth are people under twenty-five. We [older men] weren't respected, or they weren't respecting us. When we were young, and we were walking through the street - saw a Black man - saw a Black sister - we would hail them and say: 'hello'. Now that isn't happening today, and that is one of the reasons why the Nubian Men came about.

It wasn't called Nubian Men at the beginning - it's called Nubian men now - but the group started with a brother with a lot of energy called Luke Kellogg - who has left. We've gone through a healing period, because when groups come together we have our differences, and we have our different values, and we want this and we want that. For a group to respond and come together it's gonna take a lot of people and a lot of brothers with a lot of energy, and some without energy, to come together with different opinions. The Nubian Men ... went through a lull, ... [whereas before we] had forty people who used to come, week in, week out. They are still on our mailing list ... but every two weeks now there are twelve of us. I'm telling you, twelve can make the difference.

I got my inspiration from Paul [Obinna] actually. I have had an upbringing, and I am sure many of you have had a Christian upbringing. We have got a mindset of thinking: 'what can we do for myself - rather than what can we do for others'? But for us to stop preaching about: ... 'what can I do for that brother there, how can we improve him - we must first improve ourselves'. ... I have learned a lot from Paul, and I have learned a lot from the brothers in talking - and when we come together as a group it's not just the lip service, ... it's a form of expression where we can talk amongst each other and say: 'this is wrong'. When we can know what's wrong, ... it's about coming together and changing it, cos if we can't do it, no-one else is gonna do it for us.

51

Editorial unity

The Nubian Newsletter [is] called *Nubian News.* ... I am glad that the Black Men's Forum, even though it is based in Leeds, is not [only] a Leeds thing. Let not the Huddersfield man - let not the Manchester man - let not anybody think it's just a Leeds thing and go: 'let's boycott it' - and say that the Nubian Men are doing their own thing. No - it's about us coming together. ... As part of the editorial team for *Nubian News* [I would like to say] that if there's anything happening which is positive, then come and feature it in the *Nubian News,* because it's not just a circulation that's going out in Bradford. It needs to be a circulation that's going out throughout west Yorkshire. Hopefully, I say me, but I am sure I speak on behalf of the group - is that we want to do better than any other group - why? Because those groups will strive to do better than we, and it has a knock-on effect.

We originally planned to look at one aspect of our work today, but because time is short I am just going to briefly go into how we came about, ... and what are our aims and objectives. The project came about because of disproportionately high numbers of young people coming through the education system, who were failing, and being failed, not only in school but outside too, by what they were being taught in school. Where there are 16-25 year old African-Caribbean young men who have never worked, never been on training schemes, never had the opportunity to go on to further or higher education. To their credit, I suppose - the LEA [Local Education Authority] took some initiative on that, and after seeing the Census in 1991, decided to do something about it. They contacted churches and community groups, and within that, the organisation I work for, Barnados, came on board and match funded the money that Kirklees [LEA] had managed to raise.

Pupil, parent and school link
When we started our main objective was to decide what we could do to try to raise the achievement level of Black African-Caribbean young people. ... There is a tendency to focus on the word 'under achievement', [but] I don't like the word under achievement. I believe we need to look at positives - we are dealing with what young people already have. What we are trying to do is re-affirm the self-esteem, re-address the balance and say to young people: 'look, you are good, there's something positive within you'. So the aims really for us are to look at African-Caribbean young people achieving things which they have been told are out of sight. ... We've met teachers and careers workers who have said that African-Caribbean people over-estimate what they think they can achieve. How can you over-estimate what you want? If you don't have any aims or aspirations how are you gonna get any? We have a situation where one of the problems seems to me to be the fact that the young people themselves are dis-empowered, where teachers blame home. You ring up the parents, and the

parents blame the school. What about the young person, do they not have a say? I come from a youth work background, and primarily my main focus is on young people.

... I've heard people today talk about Black fathers - I think that's spot on. I can't really knock that because I feel 100% that as Black men we didn't take sufficient responsibility. ... When we ring up home, more often than not, it's the Mum who comes to the phone. When there is a issue - it's the Mum who comes to the school to deal with the issue. It's been said already but ... we need to do something about it. Teachers are terrified of leaving those four walls, and going out into the community, and going to people's homes. They may work in Fartown where we are based, but they have never seen any of those young people's homes. They are terrified of going into the estates, and going to meet the people. ... That is where the young people's reality is. They [teachers] have got to go and meet people where they are. There is no point in ... [making final decisions about why] this young person ... [is] not in school today ... [when] they have never been to speak to the parents.

When we started off we carried out a survey, where we went into the homes. Karl [Thornton] my colleague over there, was in a house for three and a half hours, because nobody else had ever come and knocked on that door and wanted to talk to that parent about their child, or about their education. A lot of our work is about making ourselves available to the parents, to the young people, and last but not least, to the teachers. [Although] ... they [teachers] might have gone through the formal education system in this country, they still need educating - and the people who are going to educate them are people like us, people like the young people who they work with on a day-to-day basis. I walk through the school sometimes - nobody says morning - they [teachers] don't say hello. They let go the door in your face. If young people see that on a day-to-day basis how are they going to learn any kind of respect or value what they see in terms of people. You say good morning to some of these teachers, they walk past you.

54

I have got Rupert [Beverley] here who is a mentor on the project, and he will tell you for himself if you get a chance to speak to him. He goes into that school and people look at him and wonder what he is doing there because he is Black. The attitude seems to be that an African-Caribbean man only comes into school for something to take. The bottom line is we are professional people, and we need to be treated with that professional kind of respect and responsibility.

I feel ... that young people are gaining some benefit from us actually being in the school - [they] ... are actually having a opportunity to taste something that ... was not there before. What we are hoping to do is to build on this. Our project is time limited for five years to August 2001 - [after this date] it might not exist anymore. We hope in the meantime that there are sufficient people in the community who want to take this on - who will actually go up and challenge the school - and challenge the education system. The majority of the young people we are having to deal with were all born in this country, and are here to stay - they are not going anywhere.

... I want to thank the organisers for allowing us amongst this august gathering - you know it's really good when Black people, Black men get together - most times it's just for a dance. Usually when we get together we're not sitting together - we are not talking to each other - we're looking for a knife, a gun, or a cigarette, or that another man don't burn us.

... The Northern Region Study Guide Group ... [is] based in Huddersfield, affiliated to Mosque B in west London - obviously affiliated to Nation of Islam in America. Mr Farrakhan the leader, knows all what we are doing. He sent a representative over two weeks ago to the Ten Thousand Man March to see what was going on. Your brothers and sisters all over the world know that men in Leeds are standing up - men in Huddersfield. ... It is like our brother [Patrice Naiambana] was saying: 'Africa is our throne - the whole damn world is our home. So wherever you are, take it, it's yours - Leeds - Huddersfield'.

Coming together like this we should not be concerned about who is worried about us coming together as brothers. If Tony Blair can meet with the IRA and he can meet with the Argentinean president, and if he Arafat can meet with Netanyahu, and if the old Soviet Union can be bosom pals with western countries, what is the problem with us coming together?

... We were at the Ten Thousand Man March, obviously. We saw all our brothers there, and sisters. It was just a wonderful feeling to be home - yet those who would come against us would say it was a non-event. Even our so called media would put it down as that. This is what we are here for, and we should not be too concerned what they are concerned about. If we are, then we speak with a slave mentality still. We should really be concerned with our achievements that we are about to make.

Our real purpose

Today is a day of truth - of purpose. ... The theme of the conference is social exclusion. I would say: 'so what'. What are we going to be included into? Lies - deceit - immorality - injustice. Do we want to be part of that game plan, or do we want to create our own? I am being controversial here, because ... I know they are listening. What's our purpose? Our purpose today - as Black men coming together - and bringing our sisters in - and bringing our children in - we have to define that purpose. Four hundred years ago they defined the purpose for us, and they brought us here. We built their civilisation. Now, we have done that. What do you do with something when it as been used and abused - you get rid of it. So be careful. Just like our brother said, year 2000 is coming and so are all the Europeans who are elsewhere in the world. They are coming back home to good old Chapeltown, which used to be a top class area in its day - they gonna want that back - and the same thing in Huddersfield. They are gonna want these areas back. Where are we gonna go? We gonna have to start fighting for turf. Never mind killing another brother calling on your turf, and you don't own a piece of brick - a stick - a piece of grass in it. Leeds man against Huddersfield man - Huddersfield man against Manchester man - you don't know nothing. What you dealing with man? We come from scripture, but we're real people.

The bible says: 'let us make man'. It did not say: 'let us make nigger' - it did not say: 'let us make coons' - it did not say: 'let us make muggers'. It said: 'let us make man' - and let's make it in the image of God man. So we really got to get in tune - God meaning force times power. Force times power - this is what you have - I have. We just got to realise. Even in our scriptures - God created man out of black mud. What does that say to you? That the first man was black - was the Black man. I know some of our people get worried by that. All I'm saying - I'm just trying to show people who our fathers were. Whose our father - who was our father? They called the Black man in Australia, aborigine - 'ab', meaning father - 'original', meaning the first - and look how they treat those people. This is part of what we are trying to instil - the knowledge of self. We start with that first of all.

If you do not know that, you gonna build someone else's reality with all your wonderful qualifications. We are all here with beautiful skills gonna build someone else's reality - we gotta stop it right now. Everything we do we must get selfish, and do it in our interest first - first of all. So do not bother about what anybody say about coming here today. 'You do not want to go to them Black men thing - you have the Muslims there too - I ain't coming'. People don't come places because they know we are there - that's foolishness.

Work equals force times distance

I did have quite a few things to say. Work Black man, work - this is what we got to do. What is the definition of work? I had to write it down because I was shocked when I saw it. The definition of work is simply - 'force overcoming resistance over a given distance'. We call it struggle - we call it tribulation. Call it what you want. We must get scientific today because everything the Caucasian man does he does it with a science. Overcome the resistance over a given distance. You need to check that ... so when you work, you gotta say: 'how far have I come'? Then you know you have worked. I thank you brothers for listening.

[I would] just like to say, it's a humbling experience to be in front of so many men. I was with the Ten Thousand Man March - it was [also] a humbling experience, and I shed a few tears on the day. We like to take a few minutes of your time to explain about the project we're involved in.

Improving participation skills

... Brother Nigel wants me to talk and then he will opt in alongside me. The project that we are involved in is trying to develop a Black young men's conference [March 1999]. Brother Nigel has been able to look at SRB funding, and has been able to look at the literacy and numeracy angle to be able to build a conference for young Black men. ... [We will give] groups of young men the skills, ... so that they [can] participate in [the] conference. That is one of the things that is missing. We all think conferences are an opportunity for everybody to meet, ... but the problem is for a number of us in our community, is that we have not been skilled to participate in it. ... [We believe that] not only ... [do] they have to be skilled to participate in the conference, they also have to be skilled to take away things, and to be able to plant that initial seed.

One of the things that we are having to question very seriously, is what happens when the finance for this specific project has stopped? ... The other impact is that we have the desire and the strength and the passion to make the conference happen, but then when the conference has gone there are four of us. There maybe two, three hundred people who need the support. One of the things that we would like to ask from people's experiences [is]: 'how do we make sure that we in our different roles can make sure that the support takes place'? What sort of things have you done before that builds that support in the community? ... There's something called, 'impact work', in detached [youth] work, where you look at the least amount of time and the least amount of work you can do to affect the most amount of young people. That is what we need to look at.

... One of the things we have got in place is that we're working in schools already, and part of the work ... is to be proactive educators. If there are any problems in school ... [they] send for the Black men. ... So we are in schools developing different projects. An example is the 'rites of passage' project ... [which runs for twelve weeks. But] we know, once it's ended and the finance has finished, and we have had a good meal, ... what happens to the young people, when they say: 'well Nigel that was really good, what do we do next? How do we get them involved in the community? How do we keep them going? How do we make sure that they understand the simplest words like, work - like strength - like unity - and to positively use it throughout the rest of their education?

- *Contribution from conference floor*
You use the word literacy - think of us as a people, like moths to a flame - we need that heat. Young Black men are already stereotyped - singled out as not good at literacy. Calling them under that banner, is like getting a dog to bite you up and then to hug the dog. The language that we use to reach out to our young people must be the language that they are comfortable with. It is just something to think about.

- *Reply*
That is something [we will think about]. We are making notes ... all the way through the conference, to take back with us.

One of the ways that we got the money was to look at it from the level of literacy as a project - which was where the money was. ... When we open up the conference ... [literacy] may not be a [separate] banner - but education will be one of the banners that will reflect that. The level of literacy, or the low level of literacy, we know, is not just determined by themselves - it's got larger and wider factors that make it up.

Andy Forbes

Black equals lack

... Brother Paul [Obinna] very much inspired us to come together, about a year ago. The group is not called 'black' - because one of the things we say [is] if you take the 'b' off black you got a 'lack'. What I think we are discovering today is the opposite of black is not white, it's wealth. If you start with a 'lack' and you feel you are missing something you got something wrong with you. You're starting from a problem straightaway - everything we need is here, within us already. The problem as the brother said earlier, is that we have discovered that we have been set a trap, and the trap is the way of thought and the way of being - the European defined way of thought. So once we get out of the trap, the wealth will come.

I could not help thinking when the brother was talking about the SRB - well, every funding that is offered us, is on the basis that there is something wrong, or we lack something. So of course it's illiteracy, or whatever else we are supposed to deliver around. One of the things I think we are beginning to reach towards is why should we reach anywhere for funding? Funding is here - why have we not got our own funding? We are constantly having to go cap in hand elsewhere. We need to stop 'lacking' and start becoming wealthy.

Self-reflection for strength

... [The Iroko Group was formed by] ... men who came together [and] ... started by looking at ourselves, from the inside out. Action - reflection. We are very good at action, us men. We can go out there in all directions. We need to reflect upon ourselves. We started by talking in the group about very basic things [such as]: what does it mean being a man? What is manhood? What is the difference between manhood and womanhood? Is there any difference between manhood and womanhood?

61

...The group is not called Black Man's Group - it's called Iroko. ... [This] is a tree common in Africa - an African tree with very strong wood, and very deep roots. What we started with was looking at our roots. All of us have passed through our mothers. In other words the grounding for all of us, men and women on this planet, is the feminine. The feminine principle is where we have started. ... Mother earth [is where] everything grows from. We spent a lot of time reflecting on that, and how we as men relate to that feminine energy outside and inside ourselves. I think again, throughout the day we are meeting together as men, but the presence of the feminine is here with us at all times. In African tradition there is not this battle of the sexes that we have in Europe. The trap that has been set us, in this way, is the European family - as I think the speaker said earlier today. I know because my father who came from Jamaica, met my mother, who is part English and part Irish, and they tried to establish the European family. [But] the European family is dysfunctional - it does not work. Why does it not work? Because the European family man has been put up there as lord and master over the women and children who are the slaves. What sort of family unit is that? No wonder the traditional European man has the wife, and goes off having mistresses and all sort of things. That's been before slavery - you can go back quite a long way - all the way back in European civilisation [to check this out]. If the European man is not leaving his wife to go and see women on the side, they are going off to see boys on the side. They have been doing that from time. We talk about child abuse like it is a new thing - like it has suddenly popped up from nowhere. So why do we want to be included in that family unit? We are exclusive. ... So what if we are excluded? Let us get excluded, and include ourselves, in ourselves.

Bicameralism

[Cheika Anta Diop] introduced the term ... 'bicameralism'. 'Cameralism' - it means the union of two things - in this respect, male and female working in parallel - separately - separate organisation - but together. There is dynamism between the two things. It's the bicamaralism that is missing in the European family - the respect for the feminine and the female - the respect for masculine and the male. Out of that comes children, wealth, happiness and well-being. That is what the men's group have been looking at. We have been looking at ourselves and seeing if we can actually achieve that by standing up as men. We can achieve that in our homes - in our lives - in our relationships. Then when we can stand on that firm ground of achieving that in our homes - in our lives - in our relationships, then we can go out and achieve that on the wider scale, in the political or economic world. We cannot go out with a very poor foundation which I am afraid has been happening. So Iroko roots and trees means [accepting] 100% personal responsibility - no whining about what 'they' are doing to us. The focus is what are 'we' doing for ourselves about things, ... instead of complaining, whining, asking for handouts left right and centre. You hear people saying: 'I hate the Council - they are racist'. [When you ask them]: 'so what are you doing next week'? [They reply]: 'I'm gonna ask them for funding'. What a ridiculous process that is. So 100% responsibility has been the theme of the group. Thank you very much.

Paul Obinna
The dream time

Last time I did a session in Leeds, it was in Chapeltown - I actually got blocked up. I was off my head because of marijuana. The brothers in the audience from the street were smoking it so heavy. I was there until about 3.00am talking with them. ... I asked the brothers: 'how much of this stuff do you smoke'? They said: 'nuff - I and I is at one with the universe jah'. [Then I asked]: 'how many ideas do you get off ganja? They said: 'nuff'. I said: 'how many ideas do you manifest into a reality? ... [They had no reply].

Do you understand me? Dream machine - dream time. I actually studied about the human brain and the masculine and feminine aspects of the human mind, and the application of ourselves in the way we do things. If you ask me to write something it's going to take me ages, but I'll draw a good picture, and it's worth a thousand words. That's a style of learning that a lot of us have. Right hemispheric children have that same thing - Black children especially - but it's not nurtured in school and education.

Duality and power

... Molefi Asante said this morning ... [that] our main intuition, MA'AT, is symbolised by a Black woman with an ostrich feather on her head - because an ostrich turns its head through 360 degrees and sees all - it's also famous for burying its head in the ground and seeing f..k all. This dynamic is there - there's duality within this symbol. The other one he mentioned ... is Auset, symbolised by ... another feminine image with a throne on her head. So when the brother [Patrice Naiambana] said Africa is our throne, it's mother Africa - it's there in ancient symbolism.

... A lot of the work I'm involved in doing [centred on] ... the education of the Black child conferences between 1993 and 1997. [It's] now stopped, because basically [it] became a knocking shop, [with] people dressing up in fine clothes and hanging out and partying. ... [When you do something] for so long, ... when it's gone bad you get rid of it - it don't stay summer all year, does it? We go through these things and breakdown and make up etc.

[Duality is] ... also going on in your brain, the left hemisphere breaks it down - like Machiavelli said, 'divide and conquer, divide and rule' [See Marriott and Butterfield (eds.), 1978]. ... What I'm basically saying is that an institution needs to be formed. That institution is not bricks and mortar - it's an attitude. You shoot a president in the USA - another comes in a second, it's an institution - it's a way of doing - it's a method of doing things - it's an expectation. That's what we're lacking.

Could I get any of you to insult your mothers publicly, no, because Malcolm X actually said the one thing he never talked about was his mother, because he said anybody who publicly dissed his mother would have to die. Could I get you to do that? When I shout something, shout the opposite.
- Up

Down
- Left

Right
- Rough

Smooth
- Rich

Poor
- Ugly

Beautiful
- Tall

Short
- Good

Bad
- God

Devil
- White

Black
- Man

Woman.

Hear what you just said, I said: 'good God white man' - you said: 'bad devil Black woman' - your mama - and you publicly said it. God is the head of this house the unseen guest the visitor at every meal, and a white man standing there at every meal, and a white man standing there in your home, what's the opposite of that? Do you need a PhD in psychology to figure that one? It's a subconscious diss on yourself and your origin. That is the African woman - which is the route of all through to the African principle.

What Andy [Forbes] was talking about has inspired me. My wife is doing a PhD entitled, *Inter-border trade in Africa*. [This] is a misdemeanour because the borders have only been there for a hundred and some years - so before there was a border African women were trading across all over the world - massive trade routes going on, lead by the women. We have been separated by that because we disrespect the feminine aspects of ourselves and the functions of our minds as men. I'm not talking about all of a sudden start 'camping' and this kind of thing - I'm talking about the feminine power that is there. In Africa in the traditions, the spirit that moves us is represented by the female and the feminine. ... I think when they break our spirit they break our connections with each other and with our ancestry which ... [is] a feminine thing. We do things in service of that feminine power, that continuation of the spirit.

[One of the things Iroko will be involved in next year is a mentoring conference]. ... Andy Forbes works for City College, and 25 and 26 February 1999 there's a conference on mentoring, it's called, *Transatlantic Problems Universal Solutions*. If you see this image [of the conference flyer] - it's a Union Jack and a Stars and Stripes clashing together, infusing or confusing, whichever way you want to look at it. There's a stylised eye of Heru the child from Kemet [Egypt] - the right eye the masculine, the left eye the feminine. ... There's gonna be a UK panel including Trevor Gordon - and Richard Majors is going to lead the US panel. We'll start looking at these dynamics that are there. Our children - you wanna see about influence - the word influence meaning the visitation of an occult or astral force. Go and check it out. Influence is a very powerful word. If you look on the head of the children, they got baseball caps - all these things coming from the USA - a lot of the language coming from the USA. When you look at things differently - look at this symbol here [Nike]. Who was Nike? Goddess of victory. Even within the thing - what's that symbol - its a tick. So you got it wrong or right? What do they say, what goes with that tick? 'Just do it'.

They are putting these symbols out on our young people and our young people got the [inter]net but they do not know a thing that they are doing. Let us energise and maximise what they are actually doing.

Some of you are looking at me negatively. That is what this [mentoring] conference is going to be doing. More importantly I think, from Easter, I am going to run a series called *the kola and the cowrie.* They may be every six months or every year. What they are actually looking at is called the genius of cultural tradition. Do you know the word genius actually means spirituality. So the genius of cultural tradition is looking at our genius that lies in the symbolism that I have talked about, before anybody else was touching us. We are going to do men and genius of cultural tradition, secondly, women and genius of cultural tradition, and finally relationship and genius of cultural tradition.

I do not know anybody who can gun as fast with personal information as myself. Those who know me [understand that] I can fire it like an Uzi - two of them going off. I can reason things out. I am wily. I am sly like a fox.

... I have a good strong woman. She is from an African tribe called the Ibo. Do you all know that you carry your woman's menstrual cycle. Do you know that if you go and play away, and start having sex with another woman, your wife will know because you will bring that other woman's cycle back. Her cycle will change. There are a few people squirming here. ... What you are going to be doing is relying on the fact that your woman is not being a full woman because she is not in tune with her own menstrual cycle. Her menstrual cycle operates as the crescent and star here.

The Muslims are very scientific people. They pray five times a day in line with the path of the sun. That is for the left hemisphere. What do they do for the right hemisphere? Every twenty eight days they are supposed to fast on the days of the white nights. Three days fast to bring in the feminine energy. ... I talk to Muslims who do not even know about it. They do not go into the fast every month. It is getting that feminine energy back into play.

In Africa we dealt with the lunar calendar. Go check these things out. It is with all of us now - children carry their mother's cycle and this is something everybody wants to overlook. We want to get back to these things because they are there anyway. They are called natural - not normal - natural. So that is what we are trying to get.

There is a term, 'foundationism' that Femi Biko [1998] is talking about. ... [This includes] one of the foundations of life, culture [or] civilisation. ... In Ibo land you have men's counsels and women's counsels, and one cannot take a move in the interests of themselves, they have to consult across. These are things we have been doing from time. It is in us, it is our genes. If we can un-block it, awaken it - we got it going on. Who has got the biggest gene group - who has been going the longest? You have the longest genetic path on the planet, through crown of the Auset. ... That is our throne in Africa, whether you like it or not. Whenever you go on crazy and say I hate Africa, it's gonna wake you up and kick you up. Don't be looking for Africans to tell you because they have probably been studying someone else's ideas and concepts at home. The only person you can rely on is yourself. So what did Jesus say - 'worship the lord God thyself with all thy heart and strength [and] love thy neighbour as thyself'.

I represent a group called Indaba - it is a small group. ... Indaba means 'an important meeting' in Swahili. ... I read it in a book when I was studying the effect of the apartheid system on the people in South Africa. When I looked at what the people were doing and the suffering they were under, and what they were going through - the power they were surging and pushing to break that apartheid system - I was inspired. I think we need that surging power ... [to] come under the banner of an important meeting to talk about things that are important to us. Not [to talk about our] opinions, ... [but] things that happen to you - things you felt, you saw and you did. [We have done this] - we sat down and spoke about our childhood, ... our peers ... [and the games we played] regardless to which island in the Caribbean we came from. Amazingly, some children that were born here and went back to the Caribbean to be brought up, we all experienced the exact same thing.

... We all know what we did and what happened to us, but there is not a forum for us to talk about it - to come to terms with it. The most prominent thing that came out of it, that has affected, men, women and children that was separated, parted, cut off - nobody has explained to children: 'I left you because of this reason'. The children are wanting to know: 'Mum, Dad, why did you leave me'? We are trying to deal with it all our lives. ... Why was it when I was looking at other children going to school, when their parents were watching them playing - where was mine? I grew up with someone I called Mama and Papa they were my grandparents. Who are these ['new'] people asking me to call them Mama and Papa?

... There are so many questions that we need to deal with [and it's] ... keeping us down, because you cannot rise up until you know where you are coming from. You can't run with runners until someone gives you running shoes. We need to sit and talk, and I am really inspired that everywhere throughout the country, Black men and women are talking.

69

... [We should make our own agenda and not look for support from the media. For example], not one newspaper publicised a fitting tribute to that Ten Thousand Man March, and should I say fifteen thousand. If someone did not record Rodney King being beaten up in America, Chicago would not have burnt down. If that place did not burn down nothing would have changed. We have to respond to every incident that we are in. We have to hit back - we really do. ... I have stopped buying the media newspapers, they are so 'heavy' I cannot carry them home - they are so full of shit. I now buy this paper [The Final Call] because it inspires me. It has international things, and it only talks about Blacks - that is all I need to know. I know so much about this society, I do not need to know anymore.

I wasn't really going to say anything, but I felt that since we have come together I should at least say something. Thank you all for coming. I wish a lot more would [have] come. We had a lot of people ringing us up from all over the country saying: 'I want to know what is going on'.

The possibilities for change

It is a very exciting to my mind - 1998. All of a sudden, people are starting to say - Black Man - Ten Thousand Man March. Hands up all of those who were there - it was a brilliant experience. Stephen Lawrence Enquiry - all of a sudden people are starting to say: 'hold on a minute, is there something here - what is happening to the Black man - what is going on here'? They are starting to ask questions. It is interesting that the Ten Thousand Man March [did not generate] any negative publicity, and I think there is a correlation between the Stephen Lawrence Enquiry and the way a lot of the press are treating Black men. Obviously, I wish one of the things that come up in the enquiry is the way in which Black men [are negatively stereotyped] ... in British society, [with] the underlying problem of racism - institutional racism. The word Paul Condon would not say. There is [an opportunity] ... now for British society, hopefully, if they take in what comes up in the Lawrence Enquiry, which obviously they will not. There will be a lot of information that ... can be worked on, and hopefully something comes of it.

History of African people in schools

I just want to say a little bit about something else we did in terms of the Black Men's Forum. We did some stuff in schools, which for us it is very important. I think most of the speakers so far have spoken about education, education, education. Educating the mind, talking of understanding your own culture and where you are from - your history. We are not going to hear Black history in the schools - it is not part of the national curriculum.

71

... We [Black Men's Forum] did some stuff in the schools - we did some Windrush workshops. It was mainly the primary schools who picked it up, and having said that, it was the schools that had the Black staff. Leeds has CPSA's ... [who provide] teacher support. They have Black men in there - they have Black women in there - but at the end of the day they do not have qualified status. That is the key thing. We need to have Black qualified people teaching in the classrooms, and hopefully encourage them to ... teach the right things and to challenge the system from the inside - which is not very easy. Anybody who works for an institution will know straight away the difficulties of working in a white institution - Black face trying to hammer away - it is not easy. Having said that, you have to try in your own way. There are different ways you can do it.

The workshops worked in a fashion - we were able to talk about Windrush experiences. A lot of schools were into the idea that they were going to celebrate the fiftieth anniversary of the Windrush into Tilbury Docks. One school where when I went in, the [Black Men's Forum workshop facilitator] ... encouraged the youngsters to talk about their experiences within school. What started to happen was the young people, the young men in particular were talking about the attitudes of the teachers ... and the way in which they disciplined young boys. It was obvious [that] the white teachers [at the workshop] were not feeling very comfortable. ... [There is of course a link here] ... with the level of Black exclusions, which remains out of proportion. For me [this is] the key thing in regards to education.

Feed-back to women of African descent
I always like to speak to Black women after I do things like this. Tonight I will get five to six phone calls [from women asking]: 'what went on, what were you talking about'? I suggest everybody else does the same - [feed-back to Black women]. All Black women are basically saying is: 'what are you gonna do'? [The outcome of this conference] ... should not be a feel-good factor - it should be a continuation of a process whereby you take responsibility -

go back to your communities and make a difference. I think one of the key things is talking to your young Black brothers. If you are not prepared to do that what are you doing here? Whether you as an individual or an organisation ... you have to go back into your communities and make a difference. So when a Black women says to you: 'what are you gonna do - what have you learnt? You have an answer. That is one of the things about the Black Men's Forum, if somebody asks us what have we done, we can turn round and ... give practical things that we have done. At least if we have tried we are half way there. If you have not tried you leave yourself open to criticisms like, Black people coming together again and talking [but doing nothing practical to change the situation].

Do we have unity?
...I would like to add and draw a few points out of what has been said. I think one thing that is absolutely crucial is if we want to market and promote unity to young males, then as older men, we have to show unity. If there is no unity amongst the older generation we cannot be marketing unity to the young generation - it will not work. ... You can talk until you are blue in the face, but if a youth can see any weakness in what you are saying they will go with that weakness. We have been there ourselves - if you want to go out and play, and if our parents showed that weakness, we would know what that weakness was - we would work at it. We work at identifying weakness. Therefore it's aright talking to the youth about what we are going to do, but at the end of the day what have we done? How unified are we going to be? That is essential. What Mr Gordon said earlier, I get that feeling it is unity - everybody is talking this word, unity, but we are not unified amongst ourselves, which is essential in moving forward.

Enemies within
Another thing we also have to be aware of and deal with is, we are talking about enemies without, we have to talk about enemies within. We have to talk about enemies we have with Black skins and white insides. We have to talk about them - we have to be open. I think it was the Nubian Men's Group that was talking about in-fighting. ... We have to accept within group dynamics that you will have some people in there that are weak. We will have meetings like this and some people will run back and tell people what we have to say. We are not to be frightened of that. We are supposed to move forward from that. ... What we cannot be doing is playing draughts when the others are playing chess. A terminology I always use - we can't be playing dominoes when the game is chess. If we are playing dominoes on the board and everybody else is playing chess we are going to lose every time. We have to except some things about ourselves - about what is around us and where the daggers are coming from.

74

Be prepared for ethnic cleansing
Another point that was made I think it came from Patrice [Naiambana], about what is going to happen with Europe [with] all these other ethnic groups coming in. ... One of the lines that always sticks with me from Malcolm X is: 'when you think it is peace and safety, in the fields, out in the open they will be digging the graves to bury you'. So ethnic cleansing can happen. You have seen it happen in Bosnia - that's white people killing white people. We see it happen in Belfast - that's white people killing white people. So at the end of the day, ethnic cleansing can happen at any time. They could come in with the coaches any night and hustle us out of our homes. Get the young people to appreciate that because they are also gonna be the ones fighting.

The 'family' unit
Regarding the family, and I am sorry that Molefi has left. Yesterday I listened to two of his talks [at Leeds Civic Hall and Chapeltown Community Centre], where he went through and explained about the family unit, how it was seen within Africa. It was the man, the woman and the child. In Europe they took the woman out of it and put in the holy spirit because they wanted the women not to be seen as anything important. Then they said: 'your religion, the man and the child' - then you have men sleeping with boys, also men sleeping with their young daughters. Then they wonder why the family unit is falling apart.

Group dynamics and the future
I also wanted to highlight the fact of group dynamics. If you bring five people together you are going to have dynamics. Each individual comes with dynamics. You bring twelve people together - there are dynamics. We have to accept that and make that a part of the unifying force to go forward. If we can accept that there will be group dynamics, discussions - there will be arguments - there will be falling out - but what is the purpose for what we are doing? As highlighted today, a lot of the time it is not about us no more. This unification we are talking about may not actually happen within our lifetime. Sometimes we selfishly argue the fact that it is going to happen during our time when we should be

realistically looking at: are we laying the foundations to make sure that it happens for our children? Selfishly we could look at it and say: 'I want this to happen for me next week', ... [but] we have to look at it and say: 'it is not about us, it is about our children'.

Include the children
As men we do not make it a priority to bring our children with us to these types of events - whatever age they are at - whether they are five years old - whether they are ten years old - whether they are fifteen years old - whether they are a girl or a boy. Facilities were made available here for a crèche, so you could have brought a daughter or a son. There would have been space here for them. That is something that we do not do as Black men, but yet still we talk a lot about doing this. It is always central. We talk about education, but there are not any children here. I think that is crucial.

Open discussion highlights

<u>Omari</u>
Greeting brothers and it is nice to see the turn out. Since I have been here I have heard a lot about things that have been happening - things that are going forward. I would just like to refer everybody to an African author Haki Madhubuti [1990] who said: 'we have to understand that we have to stop sending our children to be educated by people who do not care for them'. As the brother said, I agree with you wholeheartedly - children are rebelling and telling us that the system is not doing anything for them.

I belong to a group - we call ourselves African Building Collective. We came out of Bradford with the brother called Nabi - some of you may know him - he used to run a book shop. If 830 African people give £10 a month for a year, that is 23 pence a day, ... less than a carton of Ribena - after one year that is £100,000. What our view was - with that, then we could go and buy a building so that nobody can tell us we cannot do this [or that].

We have to come in here [West Yorkshire Playhouse] and be restricted to time and having to be messed about. I know Farrakhan (Nation of Islam) believes heavily in this kind of thing - self-economics brothers. ... Our spending power is in the millions, billions. ... Every year at carnival I see sisters and brothers with the most newest outfits - the most trainers, who must have spent the most amount of money to just jump up and down for eight hours. For the rest of the three hundred and sixty days we are getting shit. Nobody wants to do anything or be prepared to put any form of action forward. Garvey says it all. I am a staunch Garveyite, and the key to it all is, whatever differences we may have, ideology or religion - race first. Once you put that first then my difference between you, you, and you, is surmountable.

My question is to Trevor [Gordon], wonderful talk yet again. When it comes to ousting out the enemy - Black people within, what code can we set up for discipline, and for how long? People do change, they do get better and they do get worse - is there any structure for setting that up? I believe that there are certain brothers in our community that need taking into discipline, but other brothers disagree with me. We need something set up to do that.

Trevor Gordon
The first thing that we gotta have is a whole pile of tolerance, which is number one - when I am talking about exposing and ousting. You are right, people do have the tendency to change. I used to be a drug dealer, if nobody had the belief that I could change I would not be sitting here now. We all have to be able to give the room for that sort of change to take place. I think what I am dealing with - no matter that we need structures, ... this thing here - the mouth - it is a very powerful weapon. One thing I admire about the brothers in the Nation of Islam - they can go behind a closed door, ten thousand of them can be told something, and it stays with ten thousand. One way of ensuring that the people in our community who want to damage us, don't damage us, is learning to keep things to ourselves.

77

That to a degree will allow us to develop, and it will always ensure that those people are fully ostracised. ... The biggest problem that we have at the moment is this [our mouths], and it is how we use it. This is the most powerful weapon on earth - word sound. It can kill - it can shape - it can alter - it can rock the very existence of human kind. The one thing we as brother need to learn, is to be told something - to be given an instruction or to be given a directive and learn to keep it to ourselves. Learn when to speak - learn what to say - learn who to say it to. Then we are going to be in a better position to move on. That is a serious discipline, and it is something I deeply admire the Nation for.

Arthur France
One of the brothers talked about the family. I am one of those people who are very old fashioned with the family business - I was privileged to be brought up in the Caribbean. There are a lot of kids of African descent in the Caribbean, who see their grandparents as their first parents. When a child is born the grandparents take over, and we have lost that. We have fallen into the European trap of the parents' mean nothing - the family means nothing. We need to get back into ... [the Caribbean/ African way]. ... Every time I go to the funeral of an old person I feel sad because we bury a lot of history and knowledge that's not coming back. We want to have a 'Saturday Of Remembrances' where the young and the Black old can sit together, because we need to get all this information before they are buried.

The other thing is, our children are our future [because] without them we have no future. If we lucky enough, we live to become a child again, and they will have to look after us, [but] ... if we don't prepare, we're in serious trouble. I think this organisation [Leeds Black Men's Forum] have power because it represents us, and there's certain things we need to prepare to ask Leeds City Council and the Government [about - such as the education of our children]. ... The situation with Black kids is scandalous, and you have people who are making decisions on our behalf who don't look like us [and] don't give a damn about us.

... If you look at the progress the Asians have made - they came after us. ... We seem to have lost ... our African identity where, when we find information ... [we do not] bring it back and help each other. ... What we got to understand is that ... you're not competing against the guys you went to school with, you competing against guys from Harrogate whose parents were professors - that is how it is. [Therefore], if our kids haven't got that foundation we got a problem. We'll have to give them culture as well, or we cutting whip to cut our arse.

Claude Hendrickson
I'd just like to make a comment regarding the family and the bringing up [of children]. On speaking to lots of older people ... and speaking to some young people that were brought up by their grandparents, [and others] who were brought up by their parents, you tend to find that children who were brought up by their grandparents are deeper in their cultural knowledge than some children that are brought up physically by their parents. The grandparents had the time, ... whereas children who were growing up with their parents, their parents were going out to work - they didn't have the time [to spent with the children]. ... [When grandparents are not around the circle of respect is broken] - the youth are just running wild because they don't have the experience of seeing their parents respect their parents. For example, a child who sees their parent at thirty-eight speaking to their grandmother with respect, appreciates the fact that I've got to have this same kind of respect because I've got to have it for a long time.

Paul Obinna
... In Ibo the family is the basic political unit of society.

... Orlando Patterson [1973] wrote a book called *The Sociology of Slavery*, and he has a chapter in there called 'The Social Institution of the Slaves'. The part that kept the slaves in silence and did not let things out they called voodoo or obeah. He went into West Africa looking for the meaning of the words 'obi', 'obeah' - and what he found was that obeah meant witchcraft. Obi in Ibo means: your wish, your heart, your chief, your soul, spirit, mind, home, kindred and your lineage. One little word three letters. ... If you ever look at the traditions in Africa, [for example the] Yoruba tradition - there's no separation between the religion and the people. You don't chose whether you are this or that - in tradition you are just what you are, connecting with the God force. ... [In] Ibo we have the creator Chineke - the personal God is called the Chi. You don't have a choice whether you worship God or not, because you are part of God. So what they've [Europeans] done is disassociated [us from our God force] - given us Islam and Christianity and said our ways of life and our practices are haram, or evil or fetish. Why these people can be separate is because they can swear oath on a book, which is separate from them. ... A wise Yoruba elder just turns round and says: 'a lot of the people in Africa are Christians and Muslims by day, [but] traditionalist at night. [If] you go to a Ibo man he will not swear to the Obi - he will not swear on his tradition, because he knows if you swear and take oath and you go against that oath, you are a dead man - a dead man walking. I have gone into a traditional marriage with my wife and please forgive my language, if I decide to see another woman, I f..k, I die - that is an oath. ... How committed are you?

Ansel Broderick
I see all kind of people here today of many denominations - we're all different people. One thing about the Asians coming here - moving up quick - we close our eyes, it's hard to see a Black God - that image you have on the wall since you were a kid, of that white Irish man posing, that's all you can see.

80

It's hard to see your own likeness, and when we see our own likeness then we can build on that and go forward. The devil is our kids' employer right now - devil in all kinds of ways. ... It's not just about the kids of today, ... we have to set some foundations up to show them they can be tomorrow's men - show them they can hold on. ... [It is true that we're always preaching to the converted]. There's always the same faces in the same places - how do we get to talk to those other guys as well? We have to be able to speak to them with some economic power. ... [The other issue is where we speak to them]. I did not even want to be down here today, not here. I didn't care if this was some shabby old place up Chapeltown - I would be in it for me - well it's still Council but I would like it to be mine. We should start from that place there [in the community].

Another speaker
Why did I come here - what have I gained from coming here? I've been to about forty conferences since 1984, and this is the first African men's conference I have ever been to - that must be a historical first. I'm like Trevor [Gordon], I'm conscious about the converted - but there's a part of me now knows you have to work with the converted first. ... I used to be one of [the unconverted], ... and there's some people here today like this brethren, I brought him along - so for everyone that brings, there's a new converted. So don't worry too much about the unconverted. The numbers game is something I stop play[ing]. I used to go meeting [with] only five people in there - why? We have a set of young youth - we meet every Tuesday, about six of us. One of them said to me: 'you always spend time with the problem ones, why - what about we who don't cause no trouble'? He said: 'look at us and develop us and we will help you develop them [the problem ones] because you can't get to them quicker than me'.

In terms of resources we are self-financing in that we pay money in - but equally me work in a privileged job where I can tap into ... money, and I'm going to do that. SRB, Biker Funding - if we can get it take it. I have spent the last three weeks writing

81

applications in excess of £5,000 for the youths them - what I do with it is a different thing. I can write a report and tell them lies if I have to. Suddenly this week alone there's about three million pounds available to Black people in Bristol, ... I'm going to tap into that. Don't worry about Council money, take it if you can get it, because some of we have the skills to fill in forms and tell nice wonderful words, and that's what they like hear. Write wonderful reports at the end of it, and tell pure lies - and at the same time develop our own [programmes]. So there is some positives about today.

... I came to this country in 1984 as a Black man to carry an attaché case, drive a nice car, have a white woman and live big - that's what me did learn, and that's what me fi do. So I'm going to put myself in the position of the man who are not here - they're not on that journey yet, and I've not reached it yet, but I've reached that much further that me can be here. So the ones who are not here they were like me one time - so we don't knock that, we have to nurture that and try [to change them]. [For instance], I've brought one man ... [who] was not on this journey last year.

Open question answered by Trevor Gordon: 'do you think there is any viable leadership in this country for the Black People's Forum'?

Trevor Gordon
It's ... a big concern that I've got because sometimes you go around and talk to people and you get a lot of feedback and people say: 'guys like you should be leading this, and guys like you should be leading that'. Our brother Leo [Muhammad] is under the same pressure, brother Paul [Obinna] is under the same sort of pressure. It's not gonna work ... [because] if you take one of us and make us a leader, they'll just dust that individual. History shows that when you take just one individual the Europeans dust them. Europeans can't dust ten of us - Europeans can't dust twenty of us.

What we need is for our community to empower possibly between ten and fifty sisters and brothers who work collectively to take our issues afoot, because they can't dust twenty or thirty. Look at your history - your history will quite clearly tell you that if the illustrious Dr. Farrakhan did not have the protection he had, and did not have certain systems in place they would have taken him out by now. We have to be very careful if we put the mantle on one person's shoulders. ... I would like to be part of a leadership team but my wife don't want me to be that sole leader, and I don't either, because all of a sudden you'll hear I get cancer, or you'll hear I get a heart attack. ... That's all I really want to say.

Another speaker - continued the leadership theme
If you look at [and compare] American, African [and] Caribbean societ[ies] [with the UK] - we've only been here fifty years. What I'm discovering now as the brother from The Nation said, this issue to me is a burning issue, ... most of us here work within the community, and yet when we need inspiration, when we need a voice, a collective voice of somebody to speak on our behalf, ... we have Black politicians. [But] they are powerless, [although] it's good to have them as symbols. ... I think leaders ... throw themselves up, and ... [outside] forces can't stop it - like America I guess. I'm not trying to say we should sit on our laurels in this country and think that everything's rosy, ... [but that we should] create our own leadership collectively in the community.

You're always gonna have people within the structure who are going to be seen more than others, but I'm gonna tell you the truth - [too much pressure on one person], ... to an extent, killed Marcus [Garvey], ... William Gordon ... and Paul Bogle - just look at your history. Europeans will take out his own. He took out his own President when he thought the President was supporting African-Americans.

Claude Hendrickson

What I'll say to that is, a small government might be a group of people [where] each person has a specialist role. So you have education and employment training - you have a group of people heading up different sections, and they create a body rather than have one person trying to take over the whole blanket. ... You have them in a structure that is your structure. We've proved that it can work but the only thing is ... we need Black [male] support. The women are doing wonders - I'm not trying to talk down to my fellow Black men [because] I fall into the same category as well, ... [but what] we need to do is contribute as well.

- *Enablers rather than leaders*

Can I substitute that leadership word with one that we use - 'enablers'. I think leadership is a funny thing - we are all enablers [because] ... we create a situation and enable things to happen - and leaders will rise out of that.

Question - [What is the difficulty of shifting from the concept of 'Black' to African, in relation to individual and collective identity. For instance, where does this leave Black History Month]?

Trevor Gordon

- *Black history?*

For me it's a very very simple debate - there ain't no such thing as Black history - there ain't no such thing as white history - all there is, is world history, and it started in Africa. So as an educationlist and someone who likes to teach the youth, and teach them truth, and teach rights, ... I've got a problem with history.

- *Kemetic guidance*

I since come into contact with some colleagues in Manchester, and the word they use - and the word I prefer [rather than teach] is - 'kemetic guidance'. Kemet being the first civilisation - guidance being what we as African should be bringing to the youths more than say 'teaching', which is a very European concept. [Similarly] - education - EDUCATE - is linear - it means: 'to put in'. I know that inside a lot of our youngsters there's stuff to pull out, and the African system of teaching [called] ... Yunga, ... [means] that you are seen as equal to the person you are teaching. [The enabler's] ... function is not just to put in, but it is also to pull out. ... It's a two way process - not a one way process [which indicates that] I put in and you become what I tell you to be.

- *Blacks or Africans?*
I'm gonna tell you the truth, I have a real problem with this [debate], ... it's so simple. [For instance], if your Council had any common sense - if they take their own scientific benchmark and apply it, ... it's very, very simple. They're English, they don't call themselves white - they use a descriptor that refers to a geographical location. Earlier on we talked about Pakistanis - that's a geographical descriptor - Indians, that's a geographical descriptor - Spanish, that's a geographical descriptor. These people will tell you about being scientific and then they will go out and monitor people, and they'll tell you to go and monitor the English, the Welsh, the Scottish, the Irish and the 'Blacks'. It's unscientific because four are geographical descriptors and one is a phenotype descriptor. How is the information going to be consistent in the gathering of that scientific data? To me it's real simple stuff, and if people want to break it down, ... I am African by origin and Caribbean by birth. I have some daughters who are African by origin and European by birth. Brother Asante is African by origin and American by birth. I don't have any problem breaking it down for people. There are a lot of people who like this term 'Black' - take the dictionary up tonight and just look at this word 'black' - photocopy it and give it to your Councillors - it's about science and being correct, that's what it's about. They are being incorrect when using this term 'Black', particularly when they want to sit it beside South East Asians. A hundred years ago a Pakistani was a Pakistani, I was a nigger. ... A hundred years ago Indians were Indians, I was a nigger, fifty years ago Indians were Indians and I was coloured, now Indians are Indians and I'm 'Black'. So as far as I'm concerned it's about being consistent - it's about making sure that you are consistent in how you describe people.

Another speaker

The word black is synonymous with Africa, ... literally translated, it's the land of the Blacks. I have no difficulty being referred to as African or Black because to me they mean the same thing.

Lawrence Alexander

Mine is not a question but an observation of the day - what I got out of it. ... It's been mentioned before about the converted - whose here is excellent - I feel good, but I'm truly concerned that the people who are here are converted or half converted, or on the right road - but the people who are not here, the masses who are not here, that I'm concerned about. Like the gentleman said earlier I'd rather have a marquee set up in Potternewton park like a revival thing and see it as a landmark right in the heart of the community, and make people think what's going on there, what's happening - drop leaflets in the bookies and in the pubs on the front-line. I want them here because as much as we can do here - we can go and network - leave our homes and do our best - it's them we want in here as well, so we can share ideas. It's a lovely venue, but I'd rather be sitting in a tent or on a bench.

Another speaker

I think Trevor [Gordon] already said it - we are beginning to learn how much we think about things - have been influenced, infected, contaminated by our European way of doing things - the whole debate about leadership - about colour. [The] leadership image we have is a European image of leadership. [For instance], is Tony Blair the leader of this country? No, he's the spokesperson - he's the front-man. [So] whose really in power? You don't see them - they're not there in front of the television screen because they don't want to be there. So why should we have to have people out there to be shot? We can lead invisibly. I think that leads back to what the last guy was saying. I have a feeling that, yes you set up a tent and draw people, but I think the way we need to work is a lot less visible. ... A lot of work is being done not in Manchester but invisibly in little conversations on street corners and clubs - wherever things are happening.

... [People] drop little words that start processes off, to bring people to events like this over a period of time.

... [The other issues is], how we can start moving away from the conference [set-up which] ... is a European format [of] getting thousands of people together. ... The question I'm asking Trevor [Gordon] is: 'what sort of ideas you might have for actually moving things away from these European formats into something which is more conducive to our way of thinking?

Trevor Gordon
I always wonder to myself at the end of the day: 'what does it take to get the people who don't hear the message to come'? I mean it's a revelation to be told at lunch-time [that] there were some brothers down in Chapeltown who don't want to hear Trevor Gordon - because once you hear me you can't say you ain't been told. They're a lot of brothers who are in this nice comfortable place - in this nice comfortable warm corner in the breast of the white man, drawing their 'social beamas', ... a run two baby-mothers, nice and cosy. If I come along and hear a brother like Trevor Gordon I can't walk around and use it as an excuse to be sucking this big titty feeling nice and warm. To get to a point were I'm at, and to get to a point that a lot of people in this room are at, takes coming out of the warm place and going through the wilderness, to get to a place that would make a warm place look like salt. A whole heap of the brothers don't want to hear me, don't wanna hear half of the people in this room - once they've been told they've been told. It's like Paul [Obinna] said: 'word sound, word power'. They've heard - so they can't turn around and keep sucking this titty with impunity.

... Which white boys you know have six baby-mothers? Which one? ... Have you seen how European culture is so [much] about the man - the white boy gets her pregnant [and] he's marched down the church to marry her - but for us it's perfectly acceptable [to have six baby-mothers]. All I'm trying to say is I know what's going on. I see the brothers everyday - society has created a nice little comfortable titty for them to suck - make them stay there and suck it, because to get to where I'm at - to get to where half of the people in this room are at, is gonna take some pain in order to get that gain, and they gotta come out and go into a grey place, through the wilderness. [The] Quran and the Bible is about the people going through the wilderness - it's something our creator wants us to do to reach a particular point, and a whole heap of them are not letting that titty go - that titty is warm and the milk is sweet.

Omari
A reference to something that Paul [Obinna] was saying about obeah. There's a very good book by Dr. Yosef [Ben-Jochannan, 1991] called, *African Origins of Major Western Religions* - that book is wicked. It explains the whole conception of voodoo, and what other people tend to regard as foolishness, such as obeah.

[There was a continuing discussion about attracting the men who do not normally attend 'political' conferences. This was concluded by Trevor Gordon].

Trevor Gordon
I'd get 'Beenie-Man' in a tent in Chapeltown, because a lot of these pop stars, video and movie stars, let's face it they're the ones who have got the mind-set of our people at the moment. I got no respect for that person - the only person I respect is the creator. It's time we look 'Beenie-Man' in the face and say: 'come and do some work'. I want to draw certain people - you go to these rap artists and you go to these so and so's who are just lining their pockets with millions of pounds and say: 'what happen me brethren, time to do some work'. [If some of our people will follow people like] ... 'Beenie-Man' to the ends of the earth ... we lay on an event where people like Paul [Obinna] and Andy [Forbes] - the people who we have seen today - the people like Patrice [Naiambana], can get to deal with them. Beenie [can] do one piece for five minutes. ... My approach ... [is that] it takes fire to fight fire.

Claude Hendrickson
We're winding this down now. ... I'm really glad that everybody has stayed until this stage, and notice that some people have been holding up their hands, but I've tried to make other people get a word in who haven't had a chance to speak.

I just want to take something from what Molefi said: 'there's nothing more correct for Africans than our own historical experiences' - this is the truth. It's the truth that we're coming with, and that's what we've got to know. There will be people who don't want to hear the truth no matter what we say - they don't want to hear it, but we have to remember that is what we're coming with. [Finally] - what I'd like to do at this stage is to maybe bring round the group that organised [the conference].

St. Clair Brown [for conference organising group]
We've got everybody's names and addresses - if people want a copy, and if everybody's in agreement with that, we can distribute it. ... We also gonna provide a video of the whole session from this morning to this afternoon. ... It's very rarely that all the brothers meet like this, and I think these events come too infrequently, ... [therefore] we need to put something in place where we can meet on a more regular basis.

[One of the reasons behind this conference was to improve our networking contacts and to try and create the basis of a national co-ordinating committee for the various work we do around men of African descent. We need] ... a group of people from around the country who could link up on a regular basis whether by phone or passing on information [in other formats. For instance], ... the brothers down London have got a project that they're setting up soon, they're sending us information and we can then send it over to Bradford and Huddersfield, so that information starts to spread round. [Therefore] ... people know what's happening, when it's happening, so that they can support it. All we've got at the moment is a list of names and addresses, but what we want is key people who are prepared to act as a filtering point to take information, leaflets, of what's happening, and pass it onto others.

Don't just wait for us to be doing things because there's enough men here in this room now - talk to one another [and] exchange [telephone] numbers. Decide what we're gonna do - network with one another - don't just wait for us [because] we can't do everything. In our group there's been about five of us, but in any organisation you have one or two, three or four [people] doing all the hard work. ... We [in Leeds] can start the process off - we have to start by helping ourselves.

Thanks to Derek Evelyn for doing the video.

Another speaker - proposed an alternative way forward
When we started this afternoon's session ... we said, when we leave here the sisters are gonna ask us what we're gonna do. I'm still not quite clear what solutions collectively we have come to. Could I make a suggestion regarding the brothers here who I am sure are part of organisations themselves - one of the things that we can do is to join [or affiliate to] a coalition called the African United Action Front which had its second mini summit in Manchester about a week ago. [To be considered for membership] ... the organisation ... [has to have been running for] eighteen months to two years, ... and they must be African or African-centred. ... Let us not have these forums in different parts [of the country], let us all come together, and let us work together ... [and] get affiliated with this forum that is going.

St Clair Brown
Thanks everyone for coming.

Conclusion and the way forward

'I believe divinely, we are in this situation for a reason - nothing happens for nothing. ... We are here to civilise this country through our suffering and our experiences'. (Patrice Naiambana in the characterisation of General Mukata)

Following the first Leeds based conference for men of African descent in 1997, the Leeds Black Men's Forum organised a second conference in 1998. While the first conference was aimed at local and regional men, the 1998 conference was a national event with high profile international speakers Molefi Kete Asante and Trevor Gordon, who shared their experiences with representatives of men's forums from several UK cities and towns. This report is a documentation and analysis of this 31 October 1998 conference event.

In these concluding remarks I will use the source material from two previously published works to place the arguments from this conference into the context of African and African-Caribbean continuing struggle for individual and group autonomy. The first of these texts is the 1997 Black Men's Forum conference report, *Black Men in Britain: Marching into the Millennium* (Hylton [ed.], 1997), and an inter-linked work about constructing and maintaining self-identity and community organisations, *African-Caribbean Community Organisations: the search for individual and group identity* (Hylton, 1999). I have organised the conference contributions and discussions into ten areas of concern as follows:

1. ***Acquiring self-knowledge*** as means of healing internal hurt and to gain practical skills to initiate changes. People of African descent are all too eager to get into action - but before activity there is a 'need to reflect upon ourselves' and our history (Iroko Group). By doing this we are able to avoid incorrect methods and gain inner strength to withstand negative individual and group practical and ideological assaults.

2. ***Regaining cultural esteem*** is linked to feeling good about African ethnicity. Whilst it might seem that diasporian Africans need to improve their self-esteem - low self-esteem is directly linked to trying to distant themselves from their African heritage. A cultivation of a love of Africa and its cultures is the key to feeling good about one's self without trying to adopt the ethnicity of others.

3. ***Emphasis on self-sufficiency*** concerns self-organisation, self-funding and grass-roots organising and actions initiated and controlled by men and women of African descent. Many delegates who believed in this type of activity were unconcerned about being socially excluded from various areas of UK society such as education or employment. Social exclusion may be the catalyst that forces people of African descent to organise and maintain their separate cultural institutions in similar circumstances as diasporian Africans in the USA. According to Patrice Naiambana: 'when life throws you lemons - make lemonade'. These arguments have a history linked to economic and cultural independence as indicated by this extract from a recent local study.

'Part of the arguments for customers and businesses to remain in the confines of the Black community is the concept of the 'black pound'. It is based on a philosophy of self-hood and inward investment, urging African-Caribbean consumers to support African and African-Caribbean business by using their services or buying their goods. This allows business owners to prosper by becoming strong and financially viable and able to reinvest in the community by creating further jobs. This re-circulation of inward community investment is part of the process of helping to build a strong community, providing role models and assisting African-Caribbeans to respect themselves and so gain the respect of others.

... This community concept was imported from the USA and has its roots in the traditions of self-help and self-organisation as typified by Marcus Garvey for example and his Universal Negro Improvement Association, and his Black Star Liner operation which he organised to transport diasporian Africans back to the African continent. The concept is also a direct descendent of the self-help initiatives of the 1960s Black Panther Organisations and the past and present schemes advocated by the Nation of Islam in the USA and the UK. Today the issue of the 'black pound' has a strong link to aspects of an Africancentric agenda. This is a reflection of the life-style choices encompassing all aspects of a person's being - the education, social, spiritual and the economic'. (Hylton, 1999, 28-29)

Here the emphases are on separate strategies for economic and cultural development rather than a duel approach to intervene in trying to change UK institutions to the concerns of African people while also forming separate institutions.

4. The fourth area of concern is for men of African descent to **develop a changed relationship with women, children and other members of their African family**. Elsewhere I have referred to this dilemma as the African-Caribbean gender debate. (Hylton [ed.], 1997, 1997a and 1999). It is clearly understood and accepted that men have to make 'serious' emotional and financial commitment to their children, wives and partners.

5. Another issue with a long pedigree is the need to **acknowledge and support other people of African descent.** This means rejecting professional jealousy, no 'back-biting', 'put-down', envy or 'bad mouthing' others who initiate individual and communal good deeds. This is also know as the 'crabs in the barrel effect', here described by Richard Majors at the first Black Men's Forum conference in 1997:

'One of the things we do not do in the Black community whether here in Britain or the United States is to show support for each other. ... The lack of support in the Black community is often referred to as crab antics or crabs in the barrel effect. ... You know how crabs will be in a barrel and crabs start moving up to the top of the barrel and then as soon as one almost gets to the top the other little crabs will grab him ... and pull him right back down to the end of the barrel'. (Majors in Hylton [ed.], 1997a, 11)

6. ***The creation of independent cultural institutions*** has links with the issue of self-sufficiency discussed at item three. Independence means that people of African descent would have control of events in their own institutions such as: schools, community centres, art galleries and financial saving schemes or banks. They would not have to comply with the rules of other institutions.

7. ***Use of collective energies rather than individual activity*** is an understanding that individuals are defined by the collective status of their ethnic group. In UK society Africans are a negative group where racists target any individual from the group. Examples of this include the recent bombings in Brixton and Brick Lane in East London. Individual success does not change negative group membership - therefore raising the status of the group raises individual status.

8. ***Creation of initiation ceremonies and honouring ancestors*** is an important issue for people of African descent. This enables people to remember their past, history and to secure their future by creating their own reality rather than building someone else's reality or dream. It is a method of knowing and giving due praise to those who have gone before - the African ancestors.

9. ***Rejection of class and caste*** is the understanding that individual success does not change a person's ethnic origins. Conference delegates agreed with Trevor Gordon that individuals of African descent cannot escape belonging to a 'negative' ethnic group where an African person with financial wealth (or political power) such as Eddie Murphy, is labelled

as 'a nigger in a Ferrari'. The outcome for people of African descent in the UK is to work for the interest of the group to raise group status that will help to raise individual status.

10. The final issue of concern is *the importance of education* that includes reducing school exclusion and creating cultural curriculum that reflects African ideals, sensibilities and history.

The networking aspects of the conference aims were fulfilled, although it proved very difficult to focus delegates to discuss the practical issues of maintaining this network linkage by forming the nucleus of a national co-ordinating committee. Sometimes theoretical and practical ideas are ahead of their time - but it is still important to collectively discuss the issues and possible ways forward. Grass-roots organisations have a developmental logic that cannot be completely controlled. If this occurs they would cease to be grass-roots organisations and become bureaucratic or top-down management groups. Therefore, although the ideas were eagerly and passionately discussed, and individuals and groups will initiate individual programmes of work, a planned collective effort needs to be developed at a future date.

Bibliography

Asante, M. K. (1998) *The Afrocentric Idea,* Philadelphia, Temple University Press

Asante, M. K. and Abarry, A. (eds.) (1994) *The African Intellectual Heritage,* Philadelphia, Temple University Press

Auber, P. (1999) 'In Memorial - tribute to Musa Suma', in *Community Highlights,* Vol 2, No 2, May '99, p6, Leeds

Biko, F. (1998) 'Understanding Africa', Manchester, Manchester Metropolitan University lecture series

Ben-Jochannan, Y. (1991) *African Origins of Major Western Religions,* Baltimore, Black Classic Press

Bhabha, H. (1986) 'Of Mimicry and Man, The Ambivalence of Colonialism Discourse', in Donald, J. and Hall, S. (eds.) *Politics and Ideology,* Milton Keynes, Open University Press

Black Men's Forum Constitution (November 1998) Leeds

Bradley, M. (1991) *The Ice Man Inheritance - Prehistory Sources of Western Man's Racism, Sexism and Aggression,* New York, Kayode Publishers Limited

Hilliard, A. (1996) *The Maroon Within Us,* Atlanta, Baltimore Black Press

Hylton, C. (1999) *African-Caribbean Community Organisations: the search for individual and group identity,* Stoke-on-Trent, Trentham Books Limited

Hylton, C. (1997) *Family Survival Strategies: Moyenda Black Families Talking,* London, Exploring Parenthood

Hylton, C. (ed.) (1997a) *Black Men in Britain: Marching into the Millennium,* Leeds, Bogle-L'Ouverture Press and Black Men's Forum

Madhubuti, H. (1990) *Black Men: Obsolete, Single, Dangerous,* Chicago, Third World Press

Marriott, W. and Butterfield, H. (eds.) (1978) *Machiavelli - The Prince,* London, Everyman

Patterson, O. (1973) *The Sociology of Slavery: an analysis of the origins, development and structure of Negro slave society in Jamaica,* Granada

Livingstone, K. (1998) *Guardian* (October 1998)

Sunday Times, (24 November 1996, 9)

Appendix

List of conference participants

Not all delegates registered - therefore apologies if your name is not included here

Samuel Adelrja
Aidid
Paul Aiken
Lawrence Alexander
Eli Anderson
Molefi Asante
Asher
Paul Auber
Al Barnett
R. Benjamin
Donald Berkley
Cleveland Bertram
Rupert Beverley
Ansel Broderick
Andrew Brown
St. Clair Brown
Waldorf Bundy
Clinton Cameron
Topher Campbell
Tony Crawford
Jamil Chan
Luke Daniels
Steven Derek
M. Ellis

Paul Windon-Eme
Derek Evelyn
Andy Forbes
Arthur France
A. Ginley
Wesley Grant
C. Grey
Trevor Gordon
Nigel Guy
Claude Hendrickson
Nathan Herbert
Sherman Hill
B. Hunt
William Hunte
Ali Hussein
Carl Hylton
M. Ispell
Edric James
Oliver Jones
Ian Lawrence
O. Lawrence
D. Lewis
Nat Lindo
K. Lumumba
Richard Majors

Godfrey Muhammad
Urban Muhammad
Patrice Naiambana
Paul Obinna
Philip Obara-Okeyo
Omari
Robert Pitt
Bernard Richards
John Sephula
Calder Stapleton
Chris Thomas
Karl Thornton
Jabali Ta Seti
Glen Shewille
Dillian Simpson
Tony Stanley
Musa Suma
Michael Watson
Calvin Wilkes
Nigel Wilkes
Vince Wilkinson
Jermone Williams
Nigel Williams
Ron Winston

Men of African Descent
OVERCOMING
Social Exclusion

BLACK MEN'S FORUM
NATIONAL
Conference

Bringing together from across Britain, the wide range of local organisations of men of African descent to share experiences, insights and solutions to the real, and the perceived social exclusion of people of African descent in Britain. And particularly where this exclusion impacts upon the success of efforts in education, training, and employments, and upon the leisure and social life of people of African descent.

GUEST SPEAKERS
Dr Molefi Kete Asante –Professor, Temple University USA
Trevor Gordon –Equal Opportunities, Lambeth College, London
National Black Men's Forum Representatives

SATURDAY 31 OCTOBER 1998
10am – 4.30pm
West Yorkshire Playhouse, Leeds LS2 7UP
PLEASE NOTE, THE BMF CONFERENCE IS ONLY ACCESSIBLE TO BLACK MEN OF AFRICAN DESCENT

BMF
has received support from the following organisations
West Yorkshire Playhouse, The VOICE Newspaper,
the Joseph Rowntree Charitable Trust, Dr Molefi,
Leeds University, MECAS,
the CRE, Chel Community Trust, &
The United Caribbean Association

FOR BURSARIES, TRAVEL AND OTHER INFORMATION PLEASE CONTACT
MIRANDA OR CLINTON ON (0113) 242 5996/FAX (0113) 234 4049
BMF C/O CHEL COMMUNITY TRUST, 26 ROUNDHAY ROAD, LEEDS LS7 1AB

BMF   **BMF**

ISBN Registered
ashobi@netscapeonline.co.uk
Unit B, 15 Hamilton Avenue
Leeds, LS7 4EG
TEL: 07931 384 305

LEEDS METROPOLITAN UNIVERSITY

CENTRE FOR RACE, CULTURE AND EDUCATION
Beckett Park Campus
Leeds, LS6 3QS
TEL: 0113 283 2600

BLACK MEN'S FORUM
Chapeltown Enterprise Centre
231 Chapeltown Road
Leeds, LS7 3DX
TEL: 0113 262 6333

BMF